CLINICAL
SOCIAL WORK

Definition, Practice, and Vision

BRUNNER/MAZEL
BASIC PRINCIPLES INTO PRACTICE SERIES
Series Editor: Natalie H. Gilman

The *Brunner/Mazel Basic Principles Into Practice Series* is designed to present—in a series of concisely written, easily understandable volumes—the basic theory and clinical principles associated with a variety of disciplines and types of therapy. These volumes will serve not only as "refreshers" for practicing therapists, but also as basic texts on the college and graduate level.

BRUNNER/MAZEL
BASIC PRINCIPLES INTO PRACTICE SERIES
VOLUME 9

CLINICAL SOCIAL WORK

Definiton, Practice, and Vision

Rachelle A. Dorfman, Ph.D.

BRUNNER/MAZEL, *Publishers* • NEW YORK

Library of Congress Cataloging-in-Publication Data

Dorfman, Rachelle A.
  Clinical social work: definition, practice, and vision / Rachelle
A. Dorfman.
    p. cm. — (Brunner/Mazel basic principles into practice
series; v. 9)
  Includes bibliographical references and index.
  ISBN: 0-87630-808-6 (pbk.)
  1. Social case work. 2. Psychiatric social work. 3. Clinical
sociology. I. Title. II. Series.
HV43.D67 1996
361.3'2—dc20   96-15973
                                         CIP

Published by
BRUNNER/MAZEL, INC.
19 Union Square West
New York, New York 10003

Manufactured in the United States of America
10   9   8   7   6   5   4   3   2   1

CONTENTS

❦❦❦❦❦❦❦❦❦❦❦❦❦❦❦❦❦❦❦❦❦❦❦❦

To Jay Zukerman

❦❦❦❦❦❦❦❦❦❦❦❦❦❦❦❦❦❦❦❦❦❦❦❦

ACKNOWLEDGMENTS

I wrote this book during a year of personal transition and upheaval. My advice is to never write a book during a year of personal transition and upheaval. It is far better to be psychologically at peace. I was still reeling from the 1994 Northridge earthquake and other disasters that struck Southern California a year before this endeavor was begun. Another complication was that I was bitten by the "travel bug," making me itchy for adventures abroad.

I began the manuscript at the end of a teaching sabbatical at the University of Hong Kong and finished it just before the start of a one-year leave of absence from the University of California, Los Angeles. That leave was to take me back to Asia and then to Israel to teach at Hebrew University in Jerusalem.

This book truly would never have been completed on time, or at all, were it not for the emotional support, help, and love I received from the most important people in my life. Elsa Efran, for the third time, came through for me, skillfully editing my work as fast as I produced it. Jay Efran and Hugh Rosen have my deepest appreciation; the presence of their love and confidence works miracles. My father and mother, Frank and Frances Abramson, 84 and 78 years of age, as always provided the stability of family. James Lubben and my other colleagues at UCLA, Department of Social Welfare, have indulged me on countless occasions so that this work could reach fruition. Kim Cash worked tirelessly as a research assistant and as author of Chapter 8, and Jordu Schell provided the charming drawings.

But there is one person who deserves most of the credit—Jay Zukerman. Jay started off as a friend, my best friend. We fell in love during the writing of this book. He exists on every page, offering encouragement, approval, ideas, comfort, hugs. He is a problem solver, a romantic, an intellectual, and an artist. This one is for you, Jay.

R.A.D.

PREFACE

Most people have only vague ideas about social work or clinical social workers. At best, they are often seen as caring people dedicated to improving the lives of the poor, sick, needy, and troubled. At worst, they may be seen as inept "in your face" types who ask too many questions and, in the end, take away your welfare payments or your children. The purpose of this text will be fulfilled if, after finishing the book, the reader can say, "Oh, that's what clinical social work is!"

This book is written for first-year graduate students in an MSW program. Ideally, it should be read before they see their very first client. It is also for undergraduate students in a BSW program who are contemplating seeking an MSW and becoming clinical social workers. The book is also designed to be a resource for others interested in careers in the helping professions. It provides an overview of the kinds of problems, people, situations, skills, and ethical dilemmas that helping professionals encounter when they assist individuals, couples, families, or group members in improving the quality of their lives.

This text is more conceptual and descriptive than theoretical or technical. Although there are many useful strategies on these pages, it is not a manual for building therapeutic skills.

Chapter 1 describes the development of the field of clinical social work. The story is recounted through the contributions of famous social workers, including "old-time caseworkers" and contemporary "movers and shakers."

In Chapter 2, I lay down the philosophical and ethical foundation on which clinical social work rests. Except for Chapters 8 and 9 the style of this chapter is repeated throughout the remaining chapters—a scholarly but personal elucidation of concepts, sprinkled with examples from my own work and that of my colleagues and students.

Chapters 3 and 4 begin to answer the questions: What do clinical social workers do? Where do they do it? With whom do they do it? Chapter 4, in particular, presents a broad outline of the kinds of problems that social workers address and the diversity of their clients.

The helping process in which social work clinicians are immersed is described in Chapters 5, 6, 7, and 9. Chapter 5 takes the reader through the initial interview and assessment phase, guiding the clinician through the anxiety that colors the first minutes of the first interview. The reader is shown how to organize information about the presenting problem and the client's past and current history. This chapter demonstrates the way in which social workers conceptualize the client's problems, set goals, and move on to the intervention phase of treatment. Chapter 6 draws on a broad sampling of specific concepts and techniques that are commonly incorporated into eclectic social work practice.

Ending the therapeutic relationship is taken up in Chapter 7. Although this phase can be fraught with negative feelings for both clinician and client, here attention is focused on the positive growth-enhancing aspects of the termination phase.

Chapter 8 is a basic introduction to clinical research. It describes the single-subject research design, which is an appropriate method for evaluating clinical effectiveness. This clinical research introduction serves as just that, an introduction.

In many ways, Chapter 9 is nontraditional for a social work text. Many of the treatment questions it addresses receive little or no attention in other texts or in the classroom. Nevertheless, among them are the most difficult issues the clinical social worker will ever confront.

For further information and more advanced texts, the reader is urged to take advantage of Appendix A, which consists of recommended readings on research and other topics. Finally, Appendix B contains the National Association of Social Workers (NASW) Code of Ethics.

1

SOCIAL WORK: A NOBLE TRADITION

CLINICAL SOCIAL WORK

I am a clinical social worker. I have worked in a day-care center, a community mental health center, a private psychotherapy office, and an institution of higher learning. I have counseled emotionally disturbed children, adult individuals, couples, families, and groups. Among my clients are the poor, the sick, the abused or neglected, the elderly, the disabled, and the disenfranchised. Some of my clients have had more advantages than most, but nevertheless have suffered emotional pain. Although my work is often fraught with frustration and despair, it is deeply satisfying because—I believe—it contributes toward making the world a better place.

These words describe my understanding of clinical social work and its personal significance to me. They speak to the heart. Another definition (which speaks to the head) is more comprehensive. It is the definition approved in June 1984 by the Board of Directors of the National Association of Social Workers (NASW). The NASW is the largest organization of professional social workers in the world. As of January 1994, it had over 146,00 members in 55 local chapters throughout the United States, Puerto Rico, the Virgin Islands, and the international community.

1

Clinical social work shares with all social work practice the goal of enhancement and maintenance of psychosocial functioning of individuals, families, and small groups. Clinical social work practice is the professional application of social work theory and methods to the treatment and prevention of psychosocial dysfunction, disability, or impairment including emotional and mental disorders. It is based on knowledge of one or more theories of human development within a psychosocial context.

The perspective of person-in-situation is central to clinical social work practice. Clinical social work includes interventions directed to interpersonal interactions, intrapsychic dynamics, and life-support and management issues. Clinical social work services consist of assessment; diagnosis; treatment, including psychotherapy and counseling; client-centered advocacy; consultation; and evaluation. The process of clinical social work is undertaken within the objectives of social work and the principles and values contained in the NASW Code of Ethics (NASW, 1989).

This book is about clinical social work, a field of specialization in social work practice not formally recognized by NASW until 1987. Although most clinical social workers are employed by formal organizations, the proportion of clinicians in independent private practice has increased over the last decade (NASW, 1989). To practice clinical social work independently, one must have an MSW (Master of Social Work) degree from a social work program accredited by the Council on Social Work Education (CSWE), have completed two years of full-time experience (or the part-time equivalent) supervised by a clinical social worker, and hold membership in the Academy of Certified Social Workers (ACSW) or a state license or certification that verifies and regulates the advanced level of the clinician (NASW, 1989).

What is clinical social work? Where is clinical social work practiced? How do you do it? These are a few of the questions that will be answered in this text. But first we should acquaint ourselves with the work of the early social workers.

THE FIRST SOCIAL WORKERS:
SOCIAL REFORMERS AND SETTLEMENT WORKERS

Because there have always been individuals committed to helping others, it is impossible to name the first person to do "social work." Social work was going on long before the term was coined by educator Simon Patten in 1900. Patten applied the term "social workers" to the friendly visitors and settlement house residents. He is reputed to have argued with Mary Richmond about whether the major role of social workers should be advocacy or the delivery of individualized social services (Barker, 1991). This brief history will begin, not at the beginning, but farther down the line with the social reformers of the Progressive Era, from 1900 to 1917 (Noble, 1984). These social workers were mainly college-educated men and women who were frustrated with the lack of career opportunities in a newly industrialized society. They were not attracted to big business or organized labor. The broad array of professional opportunities we are familiar with did not open up until after World War I. What many of these idealistic men and women shared was a gnawing dissatisfaction with the social conditions of the late 19th century and early 20th century and a drive toward reform.

Large American cities were overcrowded and filthy. Urban areas teemed with unskilled laborers, many of them immigrants, who suffered under brutal working conditions and the consequent poverty brought about by frequent layoffs. The social reformers attempted to improve society by advocating for prohibition, better working conditions, women's suffrage, laws to limit immigration and child labor, and the promotion of health and welfare programs.

Many reformers found their niche in the settlement movement, which consisted of individuals living together in inner-city areas festering with social ills. Initially, the settlement workers focused on the narrow confines of their neighborhoods. For example, small children who fended for themselves while their mothers labored in sweatshops were taken in, fed, and protected in settlement day-care programs. The settlements buzzed with recreational and social clubs, educational classes, employment bureaus, literacy classes, and dispensaries.

Soon, settlement workers expanded their activities to wider circles of reform. They obtained playgrounds, gymnasiums, garbage collection, and public bathhouses. Then they became even greater "spearheads for reform" (Davis, 1967), becoming involved in the labor movement and in civil rights.

Jane Addams (1860–1935)

The most well-known of the settlement workers was Jane Addams. Addams was born to an upper-middle-class family in Cedars, Illinois. She was very much influenced by the political views of her father, John Addams, a state senator, Quaker, and abolitionist. From childhood, Addams was never interested in the traditional female roles of the Victorian Era. Instead, she had an absorbing interest in the plight of the poor. In the 1880s, Addams went on several trips to Europe, a common occurrence for young women of her background, but instead of soaking up the Old World charm and culture prescribed by such "grand tours," she spent a great deal of time visiting the factories and slums of London's East End. It was during one of these trips that she visited Toyneebee Hall, the first English settlement house. Addams had long felt adrift, finding her studies of literature meaningless in the face of the pain and suffering she witnessed in the overcrowded slums.

Finally she returned to Chicago, and on September 18, 1889, with the help of her lifelong companion, Ellen Gates Starr, she opened Hull House. Hull House became a model for settlement houses at home and abroad. By 1920, there were over four hundred settlements in the United States. Jane Addams went on to champion many social welfare causes and organizations. She worked tirelessly for women's suffrage and world peace. In 1931, she received the Nobel Peace Prize for her work.

The settlement movement declined after World War I. However, it played an important role in the development of what was later to become clinical social work. Its most important contribution was that it helped to alter the belief that human distress and poverty originated from an individual's moral weakness. Eventually, the profession adopted the position that human problems are caused by individual factors (such as personality traits) as well as environmental determinants (such as inadequate housing, limited employment opportunities, lack of education, poor health care, and institutional racism). This realization evolved into the person-in-environment approach (which will be discussed in detail in Chapter 2).

THE CASEWORKERS

The settlement movement was a precursor to contemporary clinical social work, but that is only part of the story. At about the same time the settlements were flourishing, a second movement, with a different perspective on the causes and alleviation of poverty, was developing by leaps and bounds—the Charity Organization Societies (COS).

After the Civil War, private charity agencies proliferated throughout the United States. For example, Trattner (1979) reported that in 1878 there were eight hundred such groups in Philadelphia alone. These agencies had little connection to one another. A shrewd individual could easily solicit and receive duplicate services from a number of different charitable organizations. Not only were the agencies unaffiliated, their individual efforts were often chaotic and ineffective. The independent charitable agencies eventually united, first in Buffalo, New York, and later throughout the country. By 1882, there were 22 COS in the United States. The stated objective of the COS was to eliminate sentimental almsgiving (the charitable gifts of money and goods) and replace it with scientific case investigation and organized and efficient delivery of services.

Service delivery, in the COS, typically meant the assignment of a "friendly visitor"—that is, a respectful, successful, "moral" volunteer from the community. Because poverty was considered to be the consequence of moral failure, friendly visitors were, by their good example and leadership, supposed to lift poor people from their destitution. District agents in the COS registered cases to eliminate duplication of services. They also determined the "worthiness" of each case, making judgments regarding individuals' capacity to reverse their "dependency". In those days, such work was called *applied philanthropy*. By 1900, when the participants in the COS movement began to realize that poverty had more to do with social, economic, and psychological factors than personal moral shortcomings, the era of friendly visiting drew to a close.

The COS movement shaped what we now know as clinical social work. Among the contributions are systematic investigation and assessment of cases; case conferences (case presentations before a group to acquire the fullest understanding of the problems and to determine the best course for problem resolution); recognition of the significance of the relationship between the social worker and client; outreach services (extending service beyond the walls of the agency); and the eventual professionalization of social work.

Mary Richmond (1861–1928)

Mary Richmond had been a sickly child, and as a grown woman she spent much of her life overcoming chronic invalidism (Trattner, 1979). In spite of her frailness, she accomplished a great deal, including transforming "charity work" into a profession. Richmond started her career as an assistant treasurer and friendly visitor in the Baltimore COS, but she soon rose to leadership. At that time, social work's professional status was in question because it had no well-defined technique or method.[1] Richmond went on to formulate the first "social casework method," which emphasized the sociological influence of the environment on individual personality development and ad-

---

[1] In 1915, Abraham Flexner, an authority on professional education, addressed the National Conference of Charities and Correction. His topic was "Is Social Work a Profession?" He determined that social work was not a profession because it had no "educationally communicable technique" (1915, p. 581). He said that although social workers were kind and resourceful, they had no skills of their own. They were simply mediators who directed others to appropriate services.

justment. Her book, *Social Diagnosis* (1917), which presented techniques for investigation, diagnosis, and treatment, was met with tremendous acclaim inside and outside the social work ranks. She is regarded as the founder of professional social work.

Richmond inaugurated the first training program for social workers in the New York School of Applied Philanthropy (the forerunner of schools of social work). She spent the last years of her career at the Russell Sage Foundation in New York City, dedicating herself to raising social work standards.

Social casework was the first unifying theoretical base to clinical social work practice, but it quickly became outdated. In the 1920s, caseworkers became enamored with the psychoanalytic approach, which emphasized diagnosis based on an investigation of the history of the client and treatment based on uncovering and understanding early childhood trauma. It relied on Freudian concepts, including the *unconscious* (see Chapter 6), *resistance*, and *psychic determinism*. These ideas eventually came to be called the "diagnostic school" or the Freudian approach.

In the 1930s, a small group of social workers at the University of Pennsylvania School of Social Work, who called themselves functional caseworkers, began to express their discontent with the Freudian/diagnostic approach, which viewed human beings as prey to the dark forces of the unconscious and the harsh restrictive influences of early internalized parental injunctions (Smalley, 1970).

The functional school, also called the Rankian approach, (after Otto Rank, a psychoanalyst and former disciple of Freud, who later came to disagree with him) adopted an optimistic view of human beings. People, functional workers purported, were not the end products of their pasts but were capable of continually creating and recreating themselves through the exercise of their *will* (an organizing force within the personality). Functional caseworkers saw people as fashioners of their own fates. They attributed pathological phenomena, such as psychosis, to the effort of the individual's will to *effect a solution* of a psychic problem. The diagnostic workers, on the other hand, believed that people were fashioned by the interrelationship between their basic needs and their physical and social environments. Members of the diagnostic school did not entirely discount the individuals' capacity to alter their environment, but they viewed psychopathology as *a result of the inability of the individual to cope* with inner and outer pressures (Kasius, 1950). Functional theory posited that the social work relationship provided the context in which the client's growth would be fostered and released. Therefore, the responsibility for treatment resided wholly with the client, not the social worker. The term "treatment" was avoided because it implied a clinician doing something *to* a client. Instead, the term "helping process" was used to illustrate that change was a consequence of participation in the therapeutic relationship. Exploration of the past, interpretation, and the setting of treatment goals were not a part of the functional school. The proponents of the functional school felt that the client's growth could not be predicted; therefore, there was no diagnostic labeling or concern with a specific outcome.

The debate between the two approaches diminished in the 1950s. Functionalism faded out over the years. However, the caseworkers involved in the debate contributed a great deal to current clinical social work practice. Among the concepts that not only survived the debate but continue to be valued in clinical social work are *the significance of the therapeutic relationship, transference, countertransference*, and the notion of *process*.

The caseworkers discussed below made significant contributions to what is now called the practice of clinical social work.

Gordon Hamilton (1892-1967)

Gordon Hamilton was the diagnostic school's most influential spokesperson. Her writings greatly influenced the development of casework theory, and her text on the "diagnostic" perspective, *Theory and Practice of Social Case Work* (1940), was a principal social work textbook for over 20 years. In it, Hamilton addressed the philosophy and values that underlie service provision. She clarified the professional relationship, the use of community resources, and the relationship between community resources, problem diagnosis, and casework intervention. Hamilton introduced the idea that in addition to understanding a client's feelings, the worker must engage the client as an active participant in change. In other words, clients were to act for themselves instead of being acted upon (Germain, 1970). After she retired from teaching at Columbia University, Hamilton served as editor in chief of *Social Work* from 1956 to 1962, promoting ideas about method specializations and the unity of social work goals and values (Minahan, 1987).

Hamilton first used the term *psychosocial* in 1941 to stress the fact that all problems have emotional and social aspects (Hamilton, 1941). Eventually, after adopting many functionalist ideas, the diagnostic school evolved into what is now known as the *psychosocial school*.

Florence Hollis (1907–1987)

Florence Hollis was an educator, researcher, author, and practitioner who, despite her other responsibilities, continued to see clients during her long career. During the Depression, she worked in family agencies in Philadelphia and Cleveland. She taught on the Columbia University School of Social Work faculty for 25 years (1947–1972). Her major contributions include the development of a typology of casework procedures that became the basis for ongoing research into client–social worker communication and the casework process. Hollis used Hamilton's term "psychosocial" in the title of her major textbook, *Casework: A Psychosocial Therapy* (1964), to signify that the diagnostic approach was characterized by the psychological as well as the social aspects of life (Woods & Hollis, 1990). She wrote more than 40 articles about casework.

Like Richmond before her, Hollis developed interventions rationally and systematically. Although they both did this with rigor, by today's standards their method would not be considered scientific. Instead, their techniques and strategies would be seen as a result of "practice wisdom." Practice wisdom is a body of knowledge, primarily gleaned from clinical experience, that is transmitted by supervisors, peers, and other experts. Hollis contributed tremendously to the practice wisdom "inherited" by students of social work. The transmission of such wisdom from seasoned clinician to novice is absolutely essential to the training of clinical social workers (Dorfman, 1987b).

Using case studies, Hollis and her colleagues regularly entered into a process of group thinking and exchange to uncover and test practice concepts and principles. This process included observation, recording, reflecting on observations, experimenting with new ideas, and, finally, trying to be as honest as possible about whether their new ideas did or did not work (Hollis, 1972).

Lydia Rapoport (1923–1971)

Lydia Rapoport was a practitioner, educator, and theorist. Born in Vienna, Austria, she immigrated to the United States with her parents when she was nine. She started her career as a psychiatric social worker, eventually becoming the director of psychiatric social work programs at the University of California, Berkeley. While on leave from Berkeley, she worked at Harvard University's Laboratory of Community Psychiatry and there made what many feel is her most important contribution to clinical social work, the development of crisis intervention and short-term therapy.

Charlotte Towle (1896–1966)

Born and raised in Butte, Montana, Charlotte Towle started her career as a psychiatric caseworker in Tacoma, Washington. She provided leadership in creating a *generic* casework curriculum. A generic curriculum consists of a core of skills and knowledge that is common to all social casework, as opposed to a curriculum that is fragmented into specialized fields, each requiring a different set of skills and knowledge base. Towle was on the faculty of the School of Social Service Administration at the University of Chicago, where she wrote and taught about differential diagnosis (the process of determining a diagnosis by ruling out other diagnostic possibilities) in casework. She also wrote about the educational process of training social workers and sought to understand differences in learning patterns of students.

Charlotte Towle is perhaps best remembered for her powerful teaching and her influence on the development of other great teachers and contributors to social work. Perlman (1989), for example, writes that she does not believe that there was a single person among Towle's students or colleagues who did not experience her as a major influence. Perlman, of course, counts herself among them.

Jessie Taft (1882–1960)

The term *functional casework* is credited to Jessie Taft, who defined it in 1937 in a groundbreaking paper in the *Journal of Social Work Process* (1937). She formulated the concept *use of agency function* to explain the reality and significance of the client's working within the bounds of the agency's stated functions.[2] She compared this process to the way in which one has to adjust to the limits or social structures of society (Yelaja, 1986). Jessie Taft, Otto Rank, and Virginia Robinson were the initial shapers of the functional school, which was to be further developed by their colleagues at the University of Pennsylvania.

Virginia Robinson (1883–1977)

Although she made significant individual contributions to social work, Virginia Robinson is often paired with Otto Rank, who strongly influenced her ideas, and Jessie Taft, her partner of 50 years. As a faculty member of the University of Pennsylvania School of Social Work, she rejected many of Mary Richmond's sociological ideas as well as many of the Freudian

---

[2]Diagnostic social workers did not agree that agency function should deserve such importance. They argued that social workers were professionals, not merely employees, and as such needed to work autonomously. Agency function was seen as simply an incidental factor of practice.

ideas about unconscious motivations. In 1930, she published *A Changing Psychology of Social Casework*. The book proposed a new way to synthesize the individual personality and the social environment. In 1942, Robinson wrote *Training in Skills for Social Case Work*, which focused on the necessary skills for functional social casework practice. Taft and Robinson are considered the founders of the functional school.

Helen Harris Perlman

Born the oldest of four in St. Paul, Minnesota, Helen Harris Perlman had a close, affectionate extended family. Her optimistic and loving personality motivated her father to nickname her "Miss Mush" (Gottesfeld & Pharis, 1977, p. 104). Most of her academic career was at the University of Chicago.

Perlman's greatest contribution to social work theory development is her *problem-solving approach*, which contributed to the final resolution of the great diagnostic versus functional debate. Perlman's model emerged from her recognition that life is, in essence, an ongoing, problem-encountering, problem-solving process. Therefore, "cure" is not a reasonable goal. The problem-solving approach is predicated on the assumption that a person's inability to cope with his or her problem is due to some temporary or long-standing incapacities in problem solving, which could be overcome. Problem-solving abilities can be developed, stimulated, or strengthened. Students of Perlman fondly recall her "four P's": "A *person* beset by a *problem* seeks help with that problem from a *place* (either a social agency or some other social institution) and is proffered such help by a professional social worker who uses a *process* that simultaneously engages and enhances the person's own problem-solving resources" (Perlman, 1970, p. 138).

Her book, *Social Casework: A Problem-Solving Approach*

(1957), has been translated into French, German, Swedish, Dutch, Japanese, Italian, Spanish, and several Indian and African dialects. Professor Perlman is retired and resides in Chicago.

CONTEMPORARY CLINICAL SOCIAL WORKERS

By the late 1960s, the term "caseworker" was obsolete (see Dorfman, 1988a, for a fuller discussion of this transition). The use of the word "clinical" to denote direct contact between the worker and the client has been criticized by some social workers because it suggests medical treatment and smacks of elitism. Nevertheless, the term has stuck.

The old-time caseworkers would probably chuckle at still another term that has come into use—*micropractice*. Micro-, meso-, and macropractice belong to a 1990s terminology that describes the size of the client system, not the extent of change. A microlevel practitioner works to effect change by dealing directly with individuals, families, and small groups. A meso-level practitioner works with larger groups or systems such as neighborhood communities, and a macrolevel practitioner works with still larger systems and institutions such as legislative bodies.

Just as social work practice is divided into three levels of intervention, the microlevel (clinical social work) has been divided by theoretical orientations. Several of the contemporary social workers highlighted below are identified with particular models and the unique contributions they have made to those approaches.[3]

The individuals featured have made significant contributions to the field. However, they represent only a small sample. Dozens of other prominent social workers could have been included here.

---

[3]Much of the information and some of the text in the following pages was supplied by the clinical social workers presented in this section.

Ann Hartman

Ann Hartman recently wrote: "My mother was a social worker...a Smith grad...Bertha Reynolds was a family heroine.[4] My sister is also a social worker. Joan Laird, my life partner for the past 30 years and my collaborator and colleague, is a social worker and her son whom we raised is an MSW from Smith and is married to an MSW from Smith...and our grandchild, age three months, went to her first Monday night lecture at Smith a couple of weeks ago. ...So, you can see that social work is pretty central in my life" (A. Hartman, personal communication, July 4, 1995). Likewise, Ann Hartman continues to be central to social work.

Hartman, a practitioner in child welfare, family services, and community mental health, was editor in chief of *Social Work* from 1989 to 1993 and has been a professor of social work since 1969. She was Dean and Elizabeth Marting Treuhaft Professor at Smith College School for Social Welfare from 1986 to 1994.

The major theme that has persisted throughout her career and is reflected in her wonderfully lucid writings is her devotion to the concept of "context." Although the theme has remained constant, over time her perception and understanding of the concept has become more complex. She began her career with a deep reverence for the social environment and a determination to keep the "social" in social work (A. Hartman, personal communication, July 4, 1995).

In her early years as a practitioner and agency administrator, she continued to be attentive to the "social environment." Later, her conceptual understanding of the "surround" was influenced by Carel Germain, a fellow doctoral student at Columbia University. Germain was developing and introducing a systems perspective and an ecological metaphor for thinking about practice. Translating the ecological perspective into practice,

---

[4]Bertha Reynolds (1885–1978) contributed greatly to the theoretical development of the psychosocial approach to social work treatment in the mid-1930s. Her Marxist views and her radical critical commentary on the history of social work were not in tune with the social work profession in the early 1940s. She remained unemployed for many years and finally resigned herself to an early retirement (Freedberg & Goldstein, 1986).

during her own "ecological period," Hartman developed the *ecomap*. According to Robert Nordstrom, editor of *Families in Society* (formerly *Social Casework*), the paper in which Hartman's ecomap was published (Hartman, 1978) is the most reprinted article in the 75-year history of that journal (A. Hartman, personal communication, July 4, 1995).

Hartman then moved to a family systems perspective. In her two books with Laird, *Family-Centered Social Work Practice* (1983) and *A Handbook of Child Welfare* (1985), she tailored family systems thinking to the people and problems social workers see. Finally, Hartman and Laird (who studied anthropology at the University of Michigan) shifted from thinking of the family as a social system to thinking of it as a small society. This led Hartman to postmodern social constructivism and her current preoccupations with the way in which we construct our context and the way in which context shapes our constructions.

Among her honors are the 1994 Significant Lifetime Achievement Award of the Council on Social Work Education, the 1993 Greatest Contribution to Social Work Education Award of the Massachusetts Chapter of NASW, and honorary doctorates from Tulane University and Smith College.

Carol Meyer

For 50 years, Carol Meyer has practiced in a wide range of settings and has made significant and major contributions to the field. The 1960s were a particularly difficult time for social work, in part because the social programs of that decade were not successful in the way that Congress and others measured success (e.g., fewer people on welfare). As a result, the effectiveness of casework was questioned. As the profession endured assaults from a number of camps, some wondered if casework would survive. Meyer wrote her first practice book in 1970 (*Social Work Practice)* "out of a deliberate effort to 'save' casework...[now] calling it *social work practice* so as to broaden its scope, and secondly addressing it to the *urban environment* so as to capture the rapid social changes" (C. H. Meyer, personal communication, February 13, 1995).

16   **Clinical Social Work**

She developed the *ecosystems perspective,* a framework for practice that "allows the clinician to view cases (individuals, families, and groups) holistically, that is, to recognize the interrelatedness of each person to his or her environment" (Meyer, 1988, p. 276), and utilized the ecomap to graphically locate the client (individual, family, or group) within its social context. She also changed the common terminology from *study, diagnosis, and treatment* to *exploration, assessment, and intervention* in order to shift the discipline away from a medical identity.

Meyer continues her determined efforts to "rescue the essence of practice from the cruel, cruel world...[by] attaching it to new thinking, new social movements, policies and other contexts" (C. H. Meyer, personal communication, February 13, 1995). Her emphasis on the value of clinical practice and its unique substantive knowledge base continues in her prolific articles, editorials, and pronouncements. Carol Meyer is professor of social work at Columbia University. She is a former editor-in-chief of *Social Work* and is currently the editor of *Affilia: The Journal of Social Work and Women.*

William Reid

William Reid's first social work job was in the military, first as an enlisted man and later as an officer. He developed the *task-centered model* in the early 1970s, when long-term psychodynamically oriented treatment dominated clinical social work. Although the task-centered model grew out of the psychodynamic tradition and retained some elements of it, the central feature of the model was in sharp contrast to the psychodynamic tradition. Prevailing practice was largely long term, whereas task-centered practice was designed to be brief— 6 to 12 sessions.

In traditional practice, emphasis was often on "underlying problems," downplaying the clients' presenting problems and what they actually said they wanted help with. For example, a male client might have presented as painfully shy, unkempt, and awkward, expressing loneliness and a desire to learn how to make friends and get dates but at a loss about how to accomplish that goal. A psychodynamically oriented approach might have focused on uncovering unconscious fears and anxieties rooted in his childhood and on changing his personality. Goals would often be quite vague and ambitious. In contrast, in the task-centered approach, stress was placed on helping clients with their "expressed considered requests" (e.g., "learn how to make friends and get dates").

In Reid's approach, there were no "hidden agendas," no attempts to change the client's functioning or situation without explicitly securing the client's agreement that such changes would be the goals of intervention. In contrast to the rather loosely structured practice in favor at that time, brief task-centered treatment was organized into well-defined sequences of activities.

These features were not unique to the task-centered model. A number of other brief treatment models appeared at about the same time. The focus on research, on specific problems, on structure, and on client action as part of the behavioral movement in social work that had begun to develop some years earlier. However, the task-centered model helped push forward these developments, all of which have gained strength in the contemporary practice of clinical social work.

Reid contributed to making practice research, problem specificity, structure, and client action more acceptable to traditionally oriented practitioners. Because the task-centered approach had its origins in social work practice, used social work language, and retained some of the components of psychodynamic practice, it was viewed in a more receptive light than when these ideas were advanced in a more radical form by behaviorists and others.

Francis J. Turner

"Like many social workers, I started out in child welfare. With a degree in philosophy, I didn't know what I was doing, so I went back to school to get my social work degree" (F. J. Turner, personal communication, June 1, 1995). Thus began Turner's

illustrious social work career as a scholar and teacher in the
fields of child welfare, family services, and mental health. He
has furthered the promotion and development of the diagnos-
tic/psychosocial tradition of Gordon Hamilton and Florence
Hollis. His contribution to clinical work includes authorship of
seven books and the editorship of 14 others, including *Differential Diagnosis and Treatment in Social Work* (1968, 1976,
1983), *Social Work Treatment* (1974, 1979, 1986), *Adult Psychopathology* (1984) and *Psychosocial Therapy* (1978). He is
also the editor-in-chief of the *International Social Work Journal.*

Although Turner is a Canadian citizen, his work has spanned
the globe. He has served as consultant and visiting lecturer to
social work programs in universities in Germany, Chile, Brazil,
Israel, England, Scotland, and Hong Kong. In recent years, he
has focused his cross-cultural activities on the plight of eight
million refugees in camps and settlements around the world. He
has urged professional social work organizations to sponsor the
social work training of refugees who are university trained and
eager to pursue social work careers. Such support would
eventually enhance the lives of the sponsored individuals as
well as the other refugees who might benefit from culturally
appropriate clinical services.

In recent years, Turner has embarked upon a new area of
research, driven by an interest in the impact of interpreters in
clinical interviews. He continues to make significant contributions to the development of cross-cultural and international
social work. He currently serves as the director of University
International Activities at Wilfrid Laurier University in Ontario
and is editor of the *Journal of International Social Work.*

Herbert Strean

Herbert Strean is most closely associated with the psychoanalytic approach to social work treatment. He is director emeritus
of the New York Center for Psychoanalytic Training and distinguished professor emeritus of the Rutgers University Graduate
School of Social Work, and was editor of *Current Issues in
Psychoanalytic Practice.* During his 40-year career, he has

authored over 30 books and more than one hundred articles.

To understand the significance of Strean's contribution to clinical social work, one has to understand the history of the union between clinical social work and psychoanalysis. Like any contemporary marriage, it has suffered highs and lows. Initially, psychoanalysis brought status to the profession and promised solutions to psychological and social problems. Then there was a period of uncertainty as practitioners realized that psychoanalysis was not the cure-all they had envisioned. Nevertheless, the union survived—with more realistic expectations.

For decades, Strean's writings have made psychoanalytic principles and concepts accessible and applicable to the practice of social work. Although contemporary clinical social work no longer relies exclusively on the psychoanalytic model (and probably never did so), the application of psychoanalytic principles has continued to enhance clinical social work's dynamic understanding and intervention efforts.

Strean's work has repeatedly underscored that in order to be effective, clinicians—regardless of their field of practice and their therapeutic orientation—must have knowledge about their clients' unconscious wishes and ego functions, particularly ego defenses and superego admonitions. Knowledge about transference, countertransference, resistance, and counterresistance is likewise indispensable to clinical work. In addition, the understanding of clients' psychosocial problems requires an appreciation of the significance of the clients' history and the way in which the clients experience this history. These ideas have been explored in more breadth and depth in *Clinical Social Work* (1978), *Psychoanalytic Theory and Social Work Practice* (1979), and *Essentials of Psychoanalysis* (1994).

Virginia Satir (1916–1988)

Trained as a psychiatric social worker, Virginia Satir was closely identified with the *family therapy approach* and was well-known for her innovative styles and techniques. She was a practitioner, author, and teacher in a variety of contexts, including psychiatric clinics, hospitals, and residential treatment centers, and in probation, parole, and family-service agencies.

Satir was proud of her social work background, yet she was vocal in her efforts to get rid of the professional boundaries between social work, psychiatry, and psychology. She felt that although the disciplines had different roots, they all needed to know the same things in order to help clients. During her career, she preferred to call herself a human educator. She also wanted to eliminate the term "therapy" as denoting clinical work, saying that therapy is but one form of human education, and she spoke of human growth rather than the pursuit of mental health. Satir was one of a significant number of social workers who dismissed the orthodoxy of psychoanalysis in favor of the exploration of the human potential movement of the 1960s.

In many ways, Satir's work with families focused on their strengths and potential rather than on their pathology, and underscored social workers' reluctance to label clients with diagnoses.

Scott Briar

Scott Briar has played a key role in the development and growth of what is known as *empirical clinical practice*—that is, clinical practice that utilizes techniques whose efficacy is supported by the results of scientific investigation (see Reid, 1994, for a review of the literature on empirical practice). Using real people with real problems as subjects, researchers determine if assessment and intervention techniques live up to the claims of the clinicians who use them. (See Chapter 8 for a discussion of practice evaluation, one facet of empirical practice by which individual clinicians measure the results of their work with individuals, families, and small groups.)

Briar's book (Briar & Miller, 1971) presented one of the first formulations of contemporary empirical practice. Later, as dean of the School of Social Work at the University of Washington, he led his faculty to develop an educational program stressing the integration of practice and research (Reid, 1994).

He has encouraged practitioners in building their own empirically based models and evaluating their practices.

Monica McGoldrick

Monica McGoldrick is deeply committed to the importance of restoring the "right relations among things" (McGoldrick, 1991, p. 5). Through her writing and teaching, she has contributed to clinical social work by further sensitizing the profession to the interplay of class, gender, and culture as well as to the profound role of racism in society. She has written about the way in which the dominant group controls ideas, values, and beliefs, thus controlling the organization of interpersonal relationships (McGoldrick, 1991).

The second of three sisters, McGoldrick was born into a fourth-generation Irish-American family in Brooklyn. After receiving a masters degree in Russian studies from Yale University, she switched careers to clinical social work and received her MSW from Smith College School for Social Work in 1969. At some point along the way, she "fell in love with family therapy" (M. McGoldrick, personal communication, June 7, 1995). She is the cofounder and director of the Family Institute of New Jersey, an associate professor of clinical psychiatry at the Robert Wood Johnson Medical School, a visiting professor at Fordham University School of Social Service, and a faculty member of the Family Institute of Westchester. In addition to her writing and teaching, she maintains a private practice with individuals, couples, and families.

Her books include *You Can Go Home Again* (1985), *The Changing Family Lifestyle: A Framework for Family Therapy* (Carter & McGoldrick, 1988), and *Genograms in Family Assessment* (McGoldrick & Gerson, 1985). Her book *Ethnicity and Family Therapy* (McGoldrick, Pearce, & Giordano, 1982) is well-known and widely used.

Carolyn Saari

Carolyn Saari is a clinical social worker and professor who is on the cutting edge of social work theory development. Saari traces

the early influences on her life to the 1950s, when she was a high
school student in Montgomery, Alabama. "Living in fear is not
pleasant and certainly not the prescribed way to spend one's
adolescence, but it does provide one with exposure to the world's
inequities and with the motivations that can lead to a social work
career" (C. Saari, personal communication, February 9, 1995).

Like other theoreticians, Saari strives to understand the way
in which injustice and oppression damage individual potential.
It was in the 1960s that she first came to the conviction that
individual treatment is not merely a way to help clients adapt
to a sick society. Reflecting on that time, she writes, "I did not
have a very adequate way of arguing with those who said it
was...I can do better now" (C. Saari, personal communication,
February 9, 1995).

One of Saari's major contributions has been making the
constructivism model more accessible to social workers by
introducing it as a framework for clinical practice in *The
Creation of Meaning in Clinical Social Work* (1991). She points
out that individuals are meaning-making beings. "What matters
in determining the client's problem-solving behavior is not
necessarily the situation in which the client finds himself or
herself as viewed from a purely external or objective point of
view. Instead, it is the manner in which the client construes that
situation that is of special significance" (p. 12).

She is a professor of social work at Loyola University and
maintains a private practice in Chicago.

Naomi Golan

Although social workers have assisted clients suffering from
acute stress-generated problems since the days of the "friendly
visitors," it took many years to formulate an effective crisis
treatment model. Naomi Golan made significant contributions
to the development of the *crisis theory* and the *crisis intervention model*. Her popular text, *Treatment in Crisis Situations*
(Golan, 1978), defined a basic treatment model for social work
in a range of settings. By the 1980s, crisis intervention and

planned short-term intervention had been assimilated into mainstream social work practice (Turner, 1986).

Naomi Golan was born in Chicago but moved to Israel in 1971. For many years, she taught alternately in both the United States and Israel (University of Wisconsin–Madison, Hebrew University in Jerusalem, University of California at Berkeley, University of Haifa, University of Southern California, and Smith College School for Social Work). She is professor emerita at the University of Haifa, Israel, from which she retired in 1984. She was awarded the Jerusalem Prize by the Municipality of Jerusalem in November 1990 in recognition of her lifetime of service to the community and to the social work profession.

Max Siporin

When the other clinical social workers on these pages were asked to suggest social workers who they thought should be included here, Max Siporin's name came up again and again. Several people said, "You must include him. He's an old social worker philosopher."

As a social work practitioner and as a doctoral student, Siporin was among the first to write and publish on family and marital therapy from a social systems perspective. He was also among the first to write about its application in psychiatric settings.

More recently, Siporin has published a series of papers on social work morality and ethics that have stimulated practitioners to consider the moral aspect of social work philosophy (Siporin, 1975, pp. 84–89) and to reevaluate social work approaches to helping clients with ethical and moral problems (Siporin, 1982, 1983, 1985, 1989). Siporin has devoted attention to the aesthetics of social work practice and social worker style, writing about clinical social work as an art form (Siporin, 1988, 1993). A book on the art of social work practice is currently under way.

Siporin is professor emeritus in the School of Social Welfare at the State University of New York at Albany, where he was a professor from 1969 to 1985.

Helen Northen

Helen Northen was the first daughter born to Swedish immigrants. She grew up in Seattle with her three older brothers and younger sister in a "rather old large house...in a multi-ethnic neighborhood, with open doors and friendly neighbors." She attributes her lifelong interest in the sociocultural aspects of life-styles to her childhood in a diverse environment. She was a graduate student in psychology when she learned about social work and its emphasis on the social environment. She immediately switched her major, a decision she says she's "never regretted" (H. Northen, personal communication, July 19, 1995).

Nevertheless, there was one stumbling block. She had trouble accepting the idea that social work students were required to learn how to work with *either* individuals *or* groups. Determined to do both, she found a school in which she could take classes and field instruction in casework and group work. This experience led her to identify the numerous generic values, concepts, principles, and techniques that could be used differentially to work with individuals, families, or groups.

Helen Northen was a professor at the University of Southern California for more than 30 years, from 1953 to 1987. During that time, she was passionate about improving the quality of practice (from a psychosocial systems or ecosystems orientation). Her work was a reflection of her efforts to infuse the knowledge and skills that came out of group work into all modalities of practice—for example, using the *power* of groups to further therapeutic purposes (H. Northen, personal communication, July 19, 1995).

Northen's seven books include *Clinical Social Work Knowledge and Skills* (2nd ed., 1995), *Families and Health Care: Psychosocial Intervention* (coauthored with Kathleen Ell, 1990), and *Social Work with Groups* (1988). Dr. Northen is professor emerita at the School of Social Work, University of Southern

California. Among her honors are the 1979 Certificate of Honor of the Association for the Advancement of Social Work with Groups and her election in 1982 as a charter member and Distinguished Practitioner of the National Academy of Practice in Social Work of the National Academies of Practice.

Carel B. Germain (1916–1995)

The *ecological perspective* (also known as the *life model approach*; Germain & Gitterman, 1986) is a metaphor and a conceptual framework for clinical practice developed by Carel Germain. Simply put, the ecologically minded practitioner attempts to understand the complex relationship between people and their environmental system by unraveling the ways in which each acts and influences the other (Germain & Gitterman, 1986).

The ideas and experiences that led to the development of the ecological perspective began with Germain's youthful involvement in the Camp Fire Girls and the organized camping movement, where the emphasis was on the preservation of the wilderness and development of a growth-producing social environment. Germain's appreciation for ecological systems concepts deepened further under the tutelage of her mentor, Lucille Austin, at Columbia University, where Germain was a social work student. She also attributed her inspiration to the stimulation of the first Earth Day (April 22, 1970) and her study of the works of Richard Lazarus (1971), Bernard Bandler (1963), and Rene Dubos (1968, 1972) (C. B. Germain, personal communication, April 20, 1995). She was professor emerita at the School of Social Work, University of Connecticut, and was formerly a professor at Columbia University.

2

THE PHILOSOPHY
BEHIND THE PRACTICE

PRINCIPLES

Multideterminism

When social work was in its infancy in the latter part of the 19th century, it aligned itself with the doctrine of *single causation*, the popular scientific ideology of the times. The doctrine of single causation states that any effect can be traced to a single cause. Many people believed that this linear scientific paradigm would provide solutions to all our modern social ills (Germain, 1970). The idea was simple: If the cause was uncovered, the cure would be revealed. Unfortunately, the doctrine of single causation did not live up to expectations. Neither the friendly visitors (who reasoned that "moral uplift" would cure the "morally deficient" poor) nor the settlement workers (who concentrated on reversing "environmental determinants" of poverty) were successful in turning the tide of widespread economic depression, alcoholism, illiteracy, and unemployment. Decades of switching back and forth between attributing the "cause" of social problems first to individuals and then later to social institutions eventually led to the more contemporary *doctrine of multiple causality*. This tenet posits that difficulties such as poverty and even mental illness can be best understood as a consequence of both individual and societal factors.

26

multideterminism

More recently, social work clinicians have embraced the concept of *multideterminism.* "Multi" suggests that several factors come to bear at a precipitous point, resulting in a symptom (or symptoms) or a problem (or problems) for the individual, couple, family, or group. The "determinism" part of the word implies that clients are "destined" to suffer the consequent symptoms.

We can understand multideterminism in the following example. Joe, a 25-year-old African-American man with severe learning disabilities, was hospitalized for a suicide attempt in which he threatened to jump from a ledge of a downtown high rise. The young man, son of drug addicts, grew up in poverty. He had no consistent parenting. He was a victim of innumerable incidents of discrimination and of an educational system that did not meet his special needs. As a young teen, he was recruited into a gang, where he quickly graduated from petty crime to armed robbery.

Since childhood, Joe had been plagued with upper-respiratory infections and recurrent breathing difficulties that were never diagnosed or properly treated. He appeared to be older than his years, was HIV-positive, and was in poor physical condition. At the time of the suicide attempt, he was unemployed, owed huge gambling debts, and was being threatened by a woman who was demanding financial support for their child.

No single cause brought Joe to that ledge. The factors that contributed to the suicide attempt include poor parenting, poverty, illness, insufficient social and emotional support, inappropriate education, and a gambling addiction that resulted in threats to his life from his former girlfriend and loan sharks.

Psychosocial Approach

The *psychosocial* approach, the perspective most closely associated with traditional social work practice, is grounded in the notion of multideterminism. However, "psychosocial" is a broader concept, encompassing a theory of causality as well as providing a clinical model that includes multidimensional assessment and treatment. Since its beginnings in the late 19th century, the psychosocial approach has emphasized understanding clients from a two-pronged perspective. A clinical social worker identifies and evaluates the "psycho" factors (e.g., personality, coping strategies, intellectual capacity, and ego functioning) as well as the "social" factors (e.g., unfortunate family history, peer relationships, and involvement with social institutions). In Joe's case, there are also significant biological influences (lifelong respiratory difficulties, HIV-positive status). In fact, we sometimes refer to this model as a *biopsychosocial* approach.

The psychosocial approach is holistic and complex, but it is also flexible. Because it is an approach that is open to the incorporation of any new useful and ethical ideas and methods for treatment, it is forever changing and expanding (Turner, 1988). In addition to research findings from within the discipline, psychosocial practitioners draw on techniques derived from the empirical research of related disciplines such as medicine, psychology, education, and psychiatry (Turner, 1988).

Person-in-Environment

Because human problems have their roots in both individual client factors (e.g., personality characteristics, developmental stage) and situational factors (e.g., environmental barriers to accessing resources), we can never separate the individual and environmental forces in our understanding and treatment of human problems. The *person-in-environment* (or *person-in situation*) framework represents a synthesis of the early belief that individual factors were the cause of problems and the later belief that such determinants rested solely within the environment or social situation.

Nevertheless, clients remain responsible for their own actions, problems, and situations. In the "pop psychology" movement of the 1980s, it became fashionable to declare oneself a victim—that is, an "adult survivor of..." In the late 1980s and early 1990s, defendants rationalized (often successfully) their violent acts of brutality and murder with revelations of early childhood disadvantages, abuse, neglect, or harsh or impoverished environments. This is unacceptable to social work principles.

Ecosystems Perspective

The *ecosystems* perspective is an even broader, more abstract concept than those presented thus far. It is a framework from which clinicians can view cases holistically, focusing on the interrelatedness of each client to aspects of his or her environment. The perspective relies heavily on ecological ideas and general systems theory (von Bertalanffy, 1968). The assumption is that the components of a case (e.g., other people, social institutions, cultural forces, and physical space) are tied together in a system, locked in a pattern of reciprocal adaptation.

In an ecosystems perspective, behavior and events always have systemic explanations (Meyer, 1988). Thus, social work treatment goes well beyond the individual. It addresses the entire ecological system of the client and the interconnectedness between components of that system.

This perspective provides clinicians with an enlarged view of the case, so that they can grasp the way in which the various components shape and are shaped by each other. The goal of treatment is to restore the system in a manner that promotes *healthy* adaptation for individual components as well as for the larger system.

PROFESSIONAL VALUES

By adulthood, we usually have personal conceptions of what is "right," "good," and "important." These values are first learned in childhood, where they are molded by the family and the larger society. For example, individualism, ambition, and competitiveness have traditionally been among the basic values of the American way of life and are ingrained in most

Americans.[1] Values are also shaped by cultural, racial, and ethnic membership. In most Western cultures, for example, the preservation of life is ranked above all else, whereas in other cultural groups family honor or obedience is most important. Still other cultures prize family well-being and cohesiveness or harmony with nature.

Generally, beliefs about what is good and right influence behavior and are standards for self-evaluation. Guilt feelings or low self-esteem may be experienced when we violate our value system. This holds true for the values that guide professional practice as well as personal lives.

Values, or "conceptions of the desirable" (Kluckhohn, 1951, p. 395), are central to most professions. They shape opinions and inform decisions in medicine, psychiatry, and law. Hippocrates, the "father of medicine" (in the 4th century B.C.), had his students take an oath that represented the medical values of that era. It included an admonishment to abstain from doing anything that might harm the patient or might jeopardize patient–doctor trust. Many of the statements within the oath are still accepted as ideals for the ethical practice of contemporary medicine.

Social work has had a long tradition of concern about identifying values central to the profession that provide guidelines for relationships between practitioners and their clients, colleagues, and employers (Reamer, 1979). Mary Richmond (1917), who set down the casework method (the first social work practice methodology) in *Social Diagnosis*, appropriated a significant portion of that landmark book to a discussion of social work values (Reamer, 1979). The core value, from which all others are derived, is: *Every human being possesses an inherent worth, dignity, and uniqueness.*

---

[1]Recently, however, there has been an attempt to recast these typically American values. During the 1992 election year, for instance, "family values" received considerable attention at both the Democratic and Republican conventions, where restoring the sanctity of the family—most especially the two-parent family—emerged as a battle cry in the war against rising crime.

Every Human Being Possesses an Inherent Worth, Dignity, and Uniqueness.

The profession's commitment to social justice and to the economic, physical, and mental well-being of society is predicated on this value. At this level of abstraction, it is an ideology that stimulates intellectual exchange and debate. That perpetrators of child sexual abuse or individuals who exploit the welfare system possess inherent worth is an idea that challenges the novice and the seasoned clinical social worker alike. For example, would a clinical social worker respect the worth and dignity of an individual who is a Nazi? This question highlights several important points. First, one cannot separate one's personal value system from one's profession's value code. The only way to reconcile such value dilemmas is to face them head-on by personal reflection and supervisory assistance.

There is a story about a man during World War II who comes face-to-face with a German soldier who is bleeding heavily (his head is practically destroyed) and is in shock. Realizing that this soldier will certainly bleed to death, the man puts him on his bicycle, takes him to the commandant's house, rings the bell, waits for the door to open, and then flees. His explanation for helping the enemy is that at the moment the enemy was badly wounded, he ceased to be an enemy and became simply a human being in need (Oliner & Oliner, 1988). On the other hand, if one recognizes that personal values would be an obstacle to helping, the ethical route is to arrange for help elsewhere.

Other social work values derived from the core value of inherent worth, dignity, and uniqueness of the individual provide the clinical social worker with more concrete guidelines for professional conduct (see NASW Code of Ethics in the Appendix to this book). They include the following:

- Seek and uncover the client's strengths.
- Respect diversity and continually strive for cultural competence.

- Promote client self-determination.
- Protect confidentiality.
- Protect the client from harm.

Seek and Uncover the Client's Strengths.

The clinical social worker searches for the positive. People whose lives are characterized by demoralizing poverty, discrimination, or disabling physical and mental impairments often possess more than a modicum of internal strengths (e.g., diligence, courage, patience, intelligence) or external strengths (e.g., a caring relative or friend, occupational skills).

Let's look at the case of an elderly woman who goes in and out of psychotic delusions but who is nevertheless surviving in a crime-infested, condemned building. Her weaknesses are too numerous to list. Among her problems are mental illness and no visible economic support. A clinical social worker assigned to assess her situation and develop a treatment plan would search for strengths. In this case, the social worker discovered that her client had befriended the kitchen help in several local restaurants. She has all the food she needs. She is careful not to leave her apartment after dark and manages to keep herself and her few items of clothing reasonably clean despite inadequate plumbing. A clinical social worker would encourage her resourcefulness in the face of illness, social isolation, and deprivation. Her strengths would be acknowledged and bolstered in the efforts to improve the quality of her life.

Respect Diversity and Continually Strive for Cultural Competence.

Clinicians acknowledge the significance of race, ethnicity, culture, gender, age, sexual orientation, and geography in people's problems as well as their solutions. They seek knowledge about the cultural history and phenomenology of their clients through study and direct inquiry—a daunting task, considering the great diversity in social work clients.

Although there is some research to suggest that the optimal

therapeutic situation is one in which there is similarity between the client and the worker (Takeucch, Mokuanu, & Chun, 1992), such matches are a rare luxury. Consider the second-generation Japanese-American social worker whose practice consists of Mexican-American and African-American families. Memorizing national traits or cultural rituals would be interesting and informative, but ultimately these would be an inaccurate basis on which to "know" these particular families. Although members of any group may share an ethnic or cultural history and characteristics, subgroups and individuals within particular groups are quite diverse. Not all Mexican-Americans speak Spanish. Not all second- or third-generation immigrants are in conflict with their parents or grandparents.

Cultural competence demands an approach to clients in which assumptions are few and are held only until the truth becomes known. The culturally competent worker realizes the impossibility of "knowing" another culture (Geertz, 1987). The goals are to continue to learn about differences and to divest oneself of stereotypes. Where appropriate, competent social workers seek out community leaders to act as cultural informants and indigenous healers to serve as advisers and cohelpers. This is especially true within the ecosystems framework.

Promote Client Self-Determination.

Clinical social workers uphold the value of individual freedom and autonomy. This simple statement is at the heart of many clinical dilemmas. Self-determination, a hallmark of social work practice, must be reconsidered when the exercise of a client's personal freedom threatens to impinge on another's freedom or well-being—or even the client's survival. For example, an 88-year-old man may decide that driving with less than adequate vision is worth the risk of hurting himself. To him, mobility represents continuing engagement in life. In such cases, a social worker's responsibility extends beyond the "designated" client. Although, in principle, one might support the client's choice, one must also consider the client's potential for hurting or killing innocent pedestrians or other drivers. Social workers are often caught in clinical dilemmas when confronted with the plight of children whose parents take actions that may have a deleterious effect on them, or when weighing the rights of adults to commit suicide to escape from physical or mental suffering.

Another value dilemma that involves self-determination is *information*. Can we expect clients to decide what is best for them if they do not have access to information about all of their options? *Choice* suggests that a client is assisted in knowing and evaluating all of the options available. One of my students was once placed in an agency that would not permit informing pregnant teenagers about abortion options. Ultimately, the student determined that this violated her personal and budding professional value system. She asked for and received a new placement. Although the NASW does not take a position concerning the morality or immorality of abortion, its policy does state that the social worker should ensure that this option is available to the client by counseling the client directly or by referring the client to another service that provides abortion information and counseling (NASW, 1994).

We must also be careful not to foster dependency or unwittingly foist our will on the client. It is common for people in the helping professions to believe that they alone know what is best for clients or that clients cannot manage their lives without the professionals' ongoing assistance. Professional training focuses on helping clinical social workers develop self-awareness to avoid this and other nontherapeutic tendencies. More will be said about this phenomenon, called *countertransference*, in later chapters.

Social workers love to say, "Start where the client is." It keeps them ever mindful that clients' goals may not always match the goals social workers think would be best. It also reminds workers to attend to the help their clients are willing to accept. I am reminded of a young woman from an affluent family who sought couples counseling for herself and her fiancee, with whom she was constantly bickering. She had had a rather privileged childhood, in which she was used to getting everything she desired except the attention of her parents. She entered social work treatment with a very concrete goal. She stated, "I want this wedding to happen." I agreed to meet with the couple to help them work through some of the conflicts that threatened the upcoming marriage. Indeed, they were successful in improving their communication skills and in diminishing their anger toward one another. The wedding took place as planned. Nevertheless, in my opinion the work had just begun. With her long history of getting everything she demanded and measuring her worth by the fruits of those demands, all of her relationships were problematic. She had few real friends, and the relationship with her new husband was hardly secure. My client would not hear of more counseling. She had stated her goal clearly, had achieved it, and wanted no more than to say good-bye. Thus we said good-bye, leaving the door open if she changed her mind.

Starting where the client is means that any counseling effort must start with what occupies the client's thoughts at the present moment. If the client is worried that the man who abused her is going to be released from prison, she cannot concentrate on keeping the behavior log required in her parenting class. A teenager cannot focus on a discussion of "self-esteem" if he fears being forced to join a gang. A man whose wife has died cannot date until *he* is ready, despite the number of years that have passed since the loss.

Protect Confidentiality.

The helping relationship is a confidential one. Except under certain circumstances in which a life is in danger, such as in suicide, suspicion of child abuse, and threat of harm to others, confidentiality is maintained. When clients choose to share intimate details of their lives, that information will not be revealed to others without the client's written consent. During supervision, case details should be disguised. Cases should not be discussed between social workers and other involved professionals in elevators, corridors, or on the street. Practitioners must consult their state licensure boards for regulations about child clients, court subpoenas, and the like. (See Chapter 9 about court subpoenas and confidentiality.)

Protect the Client from Harm.

Social workers should constantly monitor their own behavior and emotional reactions, being ever vigilant to achieve greater self-awareness so that their interventions are in the clients' best interest and are not driven by their own needs. Even seasoned clinicians continue supervision (often peer consultation) to alert them to their blind spots and biases.

Protecting clients from harm includes seeking consultation or referring clients to other clinicians when the social worker does not have the necessary expertise to assist those clients (see NASW ethical code in the Appendix). Clinical social workers also have a duty to warn others of impending violence by their clients (see Chapter 9).

Recently, one of my students, Susan, was faced with a dilemma that involved forcing her to consider her value orientation. Her practicum was at the state youth authority. Her client, Carlos, was serving time for manslaughter. Carlos had completed his high school equivalency exams and was starting college-level correspondence courses. More importantly, he was taking responsibility for his crime and was showing signs of genuine rehabilitation. Unfortunately, he was witness to a gang incident inside the walls of the youth authority. Another youth was beaten to death by several gang members. Carlos was not present during the beating. He was not even aware that it had occurred, but he did see the youth being dragged from his bed by others. At first, the victim was reported as missing, and it was presumed that he had escaped. Twenty-four hours later, the body was found on the grounds, and an investigation began. Carlos confided in Susan about what he had seen. He chose not to report his information because it would mean retaliation from the gang—and certain injury or death.

Actually, Carlos was in grave danger even if he remained silent. If Susan reported the information, the gang members would know where the information came from, and Carlos would still be in danger. Nor did doing nothing protect him. If the investigation pointed to the responsible juveniles, those youths would suspect Carlos of snitching. Removing Carlos to another facility or placing him under protective care was no guarantee of his safety. Such actions would also suggest that Carlos had snitched. The gang had tentacles in every juvenile and adult facility in the state. Susan wanted to respect Carlos's choice and maintain confidentiality, but ultimately protecting him became her primary concern. She did what was necessary to place him in the most secure protective custody.

SOCIAL WORK PRINCIPLES AND VALUES IN ACTION

The following example illustrates the way in which the traditional social work value base and philosophy was actualized in response to a major urban crisis.

Civil Unrest in Los Angeles

In the spring of 1992, civil unrest broke out in the streets of South Central Los Angeles and spread to sections north and west of the city. Fires were ignited, businesses were looted and burned, 45 lives were lost, millions of dollars worth of property was destroyed. For weeks following the three days of civil unrest, people felt uneasy, fearing that at any moment the violence and the fires could be rekindled.

Many Los Angeles citizens were angered at the not-guilty decision (by an all-white jury) that freed the four white law-enforcement officers who beat African-American motorist Rodney King. Although many people understood the sense of injustice and demoralization experienced in the African-American community, few sympathized with or supported the subsequent rioting. For a time, many whites, empathic to the outrage over the not-guilty decision, felt uncomfortable and embarrassed with their African-American coworkers, friends, and neighbors.[2] African Americans reported similar feelings toward their white friends. Uncomfortable looks were exchanged between many blacks and whites on buses and in other public places. A defeated city was filled with fear, remorse, guilt, embarrassment, confusion, and anger. Los Angeles social workers responded to the crisis in a way that illuminates the social work value base.

The Social Work Response

Within days of the civil unrest, a meeting took place between representatives of the University of California, Los Angeles (UCLA), School of Social Welfare and KCET-TV (the public television station for central and southern California). The two organizations agreed on a project to ease the tensions in the city—a temporary crisis hotline. Local viewers were invited to telephone the TV station and talk about their feelings. The station provided the phones, the refreshments, and the technical support. Clinical social workers from the UCLA School of Social Welfare and the Los Angeles community took the phone lines. Over a 10-day period, two thousand calls were taken.

The hotline is an exemplar of social work principles and values in action. Adhering to the belief that every human being possesses an inherent worth, dignity, and uniqueness, social workers on the hotline provided supportive dialogue to *anyone* in the city who phoned in. Callers included looters spewing frustration and rage at the court decision, as well as terrified homebound elderly people seeking reassurance. A grandmother "ashamed" of the behavior of "my people" telephoned. A suicidal Korean-American merchant who had "lost everything" called.

Callers were encouraged to express their feelings. The social workers on the line sought and mobilized strengths and attempted to instill a sense of normalization. They comforted,

---

[2]The perpetrators and victims of the Los Angeles riots were not delimited by racial lines. They came from several minority groups, not just African Americans.

while encouraging the callers to clean up, seek resources, and rebuild.

Bilingual workers were assigned to each shift. If a caller spoke in a language other than English, the social worker on the line held up a placard that alerted the others that a Spanish- or Korean-speaking social worker was needed. Sometimes the request was for a woman or for a "young black guy."

Referrals for food, clothing, and counseling were given. The counsel to "start where the client is" was given a severe test. Sometimes, "where the client was" was hate and bigotry. The social workers listened (recognizing and controlling their emotional responses) and attempted to diffuse the callers' rage, sometimes offering alternative viewpoints. Social workers were careful to avoid engaging in angry rebuttals, which are rarely therapeutic and serve the social workers' needs more than the clients' needs. No names or addresses were recorded. Great care was taken to ensure that the calls were confidential.

To give the workers an opportunity to reflect on their own feelings, which ranged from exhilaration to anxiety, each shift ended with a debriefing. These debriefings were supervised by seasoned clinicians who were cognizant of demands of the hotline and the personal traumas experienced by Los Angeles social workers (Maki, Inglehart, Nakamura, & Nunn, 1994).

A PROFESSION THAT REFUSES TO STAND STILL

In the real world, social work principles and values cannot serve as the sole solutions to ethical social work dilemmas. They would suffice only if clinicians worked with machines and widgets instead of human beings. In some situations, self-determination has primacy, while in other situations protection from harm takes precedence. Social work has not yet defined its method for choosing one value over another in specific cases. Sometimes a decision is based on intuition, clinical wisdom, or judgment; at other points it is based on empirical research.

Social work practice is constantly complicated and challenged by political and economic fluctuations and popular trends. For example, 10 years ago there were no surrogate mothers or suicide machines. Because human problems are so complex, clinical social workers find themselves assuming a plethora of roles in a variety of settings. The next chapter will explore these roles and diverse settings.

3

ROLES AND
PRACTICE SETTINGS

Many clinical social workers refer to themselves as *psycho-therapists*—that is, practitioners who treat emotional or mental disorders psychologically, especially through verbal communication (sometimes referred to as the "talking cure"). In most cases, that term does not fully describe their work. Social work clinicians juggle numerous roles; psychotherapy is only one. The nature and number of these roles depends on where a clinician practices, the therapeutic goals, and the client population. In reality, clinical social work is "psychotherapy plus" (Hollis, 1972).

ROLES

Broker

The role of broker is a simple one. The clinical social worker links clients with the resources they need. Social workers are familiar with community resources and their eligibility criteria. For example, the client is ill with AIDS. He wants to stay at home as long as possible. It seems reasonable to do so. A steady stream of friends visits every evening. They prepare meals, do laundry and light housework, and walk his dog. The problem is that no one is available to help him during the day. The client can no longer drive or take public transportation to the medical clinic or to his weekly support meetings. Nor can he walk his dog during the day. The client is afraid that he will have to give up his beloved pet and move into a nursing home. When his social worker hears about his concerns, she contacts two volunteer groups. Volunteers in one group drive AIDS patients to medical and counseling appointments. The other group sends out volunteers to take care of pets (see Exhibit 3.1).

Advocate

The advocate role is closely related to the broker role. However, advocating requires more than locating resources. Workers in the advocate role speak up and speak out. They make impassioned pleas for their clients in the courtroom, with police, or with school personnel.

Exhibit 3.1. AIDS patient as a recipient of volunteer services—one volunteer walks his dog, another drives him to the clinic.

I recall a dramatic example of the significance of the advocacy role. Regulations in nursing homes in California stipulate periodic interdisciplinary case review meetings. Residents are invited to at least a portion of the conference. This is done ostensibly to receive residents' input in decision making, obtain feedback about care, and respond to residents' questions. On the day I visited, the first case was an elderly retired physician who, to say the least, was displeased about the quality of his care. Admittedly, his personality was far from pleasing, and he maintained a superior attitude toward the staff. Nevertheless, his complaints were dismissed summarily and he was wheeled out of the room unsatisfied and grumbling.

The second elderly resident, a woman, was new to the facility. She was accompanied by a social worker who had been engaged by the resident's family to assist her in the transition from independent apartment living to living in an institution. The social worker spoke assertively in the client's behalf, holding the professionals accountable for promised rehabilitation services. She made sure that the client's concerns were understood, responded to, and documented. Because there will always be clients who (by virtue of their disability or age) will not be treated with respect, advocacy will continue to be an important social work function.

Clinical social workers advocate at the microlevel (for individuals, families, or small groups). Other social workers advocate at the macrolevel. Macro-advocacy involves working on behalf of large groups of people who share a common problem, such as the homeless, welfare mothers, or people who are HIV-positive. In the role of the advocate, the clinician seeks to extricate services, resources, and entitlements that clients would not be able to obtain on their own. Sometimes it takes "pull." Other times it takes "push."

Educator

Imparting information and teaching skills to clients is part of nearly every therapeutic intervention. For instance, social workers teach 18-year-old newly emancipated foster children the independent living skills they will need to survive on their own. They teach parenting skills to mothers and fathers. In medical settings, they teach individuals about their diseases. They teach strategies for coping with anxiety or fear. They demonstrate problem-solving techniques. They instruct families and couples on ways to communicate more effectively. Social workers are aware that *reframing* therapy as education often makes counseling more acceptable and avoids the stigma of mental illness (Dorfman, 1987a).

reframing therapy as "education"

Enabler

The client must *do* the work of problem solving and change, but the social worker—in the role of enabler—creates the conditions and the environment in which change occurs. Enabling social workers convey hope and encouragement. They may offer suggestions and advice. They keep the client "on track," focusing on original goals and reducing them to manageable subgoals. The social worker who conducts groups or counsels couples or families is frequently in the enabling role. For example, many family members have a great deal of difficulty communicating with each other in productive ways. They interrupt each other. They may speak for one another. They misunderstand or "crystal ball" (i.e., assume that they know what the other really wants or needs without bothering to ask). The social worker in the enabler role conducting a family session is like a traffic cop directing the communication (see Exhibit 3.2)

Case Manager

Clients frequently require a host of ongoing services to live in the community. An example would be a severely developmentally disabled child. Like any child, the disabled child has educational, physical, emotional, health, and social needs. Physical therapy, individual tutoring, and monthly respite for the family are among the required services. In the case manager role, the clinical social worker assesses the needs of the youngster and the family and procures, organizes, and coordinates

Exhibit 3.2. The social worker as enabler.

delivery of those services. This role calls for managerial skills, assertiveness, and attention to detail. The case manager also monitors the delivery of services, making certain that what is received is what was ordered and that the quality is maintained and calibrated to the child's changing demands. The clinical social worker then helps the client and the family accept services and adhere to the recommended treatment plan.

Counselor

This book focuses on counseling, the most visible role of the clinical social worker. The way in which this role is carried out is dependent on the theoretical orientation of the worker. No matter what role or combination of roles the social worker is playing, basic counseling roles are demanded. (See Shulman, 1992, for an excellent text on counseling skills.) Those skills include active listening and empathy. In order to perform this role, the social worker needs (a) a knowledge of human behavior and an understanding of how the social environment impacts on people, (b) an ability to assess client needs and functioning and make judgments about what interventions can help clients deal with these stresses, (c) skill in applying intervention techniques, and (d) the ability to guide clients through the change process (Sheafor, Horejsi, & Horejsi, 1994).

Mediator

Opportunities to perform in a mediator role occur in all types of clinical social work. The mediator helps settle disputes between conflicting parties and restores communication between them. In the example above, a developmentally delayed child required services from numerous agencies and institutions. Conflict could emerge between any of the providers, as well as between the provider and the family. Social workers also mediate disputes between clients and landlords. They may intervene in disputes between clients and public assistance providers or between members of the same family (e.g., regarding divorce settlements, child custody, or responsibility for care of elderly parents).

Clinical social workers have been particularly active as mediators, and mediation has come to be considered a social work intervention or "method." Consequently, there is a growing number of social workers who devote their entire practice to mediation activities. Formal mediation or conflict-resolution training is showing up in social work curricula and is available in professional seminars and workshops. In response to the growth of this role, the NASW has developed _Standards of Practice for Social Work Mediators_ (NASW, 1991).

Consultant

The clinical social worker who wears the consultant hat provides information and advice to individuals, agencies, institutions, and so on. The advice is based on the clinician's specialized knowledge of or experience in, for instance, a particular problem area, client population, or practice method.

For example, a corporation wanted to develop an intergenerational day-care facility for the dependents of their employees. They needed advice about how to organize a stimulating program that would meet the physical, mental, and emotional needs of infants, toddlers, and older adults. A clinical social worker with expertise in both gerontology and infant and child development was consulted.

Researcher/Evaluator

Social workers assume a research role each time they critically review the clinical research literature and make judgments on the utility of various interventions. The clinician/researcher monitors the progress of clients and evaluates the outcome of his or her own work. Chapter 8 will discuss the single-subject design, a research methodology common to clinical research and practice evaluation.

PRACTICE SETTINGS

One of the most attractive aspects of clinical social work is that one can practice in a variety of agencies and institutions, including independent private practice.[1] The settings below are ones in which clinical social workers are commonly employed, but it is by no means a comprehensive list. For example, I know a clinical social worker who works in the community-relations department of a public radio station, and another who works alongside a physician in a private medical practice. I also know a social work clinician who has developed a practice exclusively for attorneys who are facing malpractice suits or who are

---

[1]Some texts will differentiate clinical social workers from those who practice in schools, prisons, hospitals, child protection services, and so on. However, in this text, clinical social workers are defined as professionally trained social workers who work directly with clients (individuals, families, small groups), using counseling skills and therapeutic methods to improve the quality of their client's lives. They may work in many different settings.

burned out by overwork or the stress of being a member of a much-maligned profession.

Elementary and Secondary Schools

School social workers work with teachers, principals, and guidance counselors to help students whose problems (e.g., habitual truancy, pregnancy, misbehavior) are interfering with their learning or socialization. Their major function is to bridge the gap in communication between the school and home and to help each exert the most positive influence on the child (Hopke, 1990). They develop therapeutic programs (e.g., support groups for children of divorcing parents) and provide counseling to children and their families. For example, a teacher might ask a school social worker for advice about managing a withdrawn child who has been traumatized by abuse or neglect. School social workers can also be found in special-education placement centers and Head Start or other early intervention programs.

Child Day Care

The clinical tasks at a child day-care center are similar to those in a school setting for older children. The social worker is the link between the center and the parents, assisting the child-care workers and teachers in managing children's emotional and behavioral problems. The worker assesses situations in the nursery and the classroom, using knowledge of human development and psychosocial factors to plan interventions.

I can recall an example from my clinical work in a child day-care center. It was 1984. The day-care center where I worked was located in the heart of a Philadelphia neighborhood that had a large population of recent Soviet immigrants. A number of problems with the Russian children left the child-care workers and teachers puzzled. The children often came to school overdressed. They wore several layers of clothing on even the warmest days. Despite profuse sweating and obvious discomfort, they refused to remove any clothing, nor would the parents heed our requests for lighter garments. In addition, children were brought to day care who were sick and feverish. When the nurse would call the parents to pick up a sick child, the parents would become incensed. It was not uncommon to have to make several calls to get a parent to pick up a child.

It was our policy to inform parents of behavior problems or obviously troubled youngsters. Most parents were grateful for the feedback, often requesting our advice. This was not the case with the Russian parents. They would become highly defensive and refuse to consider that their children might have a problem. After consultation with other colleagues who had experience with this immigrant population, I understood that the issues could be explained by cultural differences. Russian parents tend to be quite overprotective of their children. Their concern for their children's health—and the cold winters they had been accustomed to—accounted for the extra layers of clothing. This, of course, seemed strange in light of the fact that they wanted to leave their sick children in our care. However, this made sense when I discovered that child-care centers in what used to be the Soviet Union were equipped with medical staff and beds to accommodate sick children. The parents had assumed that medical care was available. They did not understand why we refused their ill children.

As for the behavior issues, I discovered that the parents saw us as authority figures. They were not used to cooperating with authority. In addition, there was a tremendous stigma attached to emotional problems or mental illness. Any suggestion of emotional disturbance was vehemently defended against.

The good news is that with time and careful rapport building, we were able to help these families adjust to American culture in a way that was beneficial for every member of the family as well as to the day-care center.

Personnel Offices/Employee Assistance Programs

A growing practice area is in employee assistance programs (EAPs). EAP clinical social workers are employed by a business or union. The scope of duties ranges from helping an executive cope with the stress of an impending takeover to counseling for individual problems that are affecting the quality of an employee's work. EAP workers lead groups on stress reduction, time management, coping with layoffs, and so forth. Among the problems that EAP workers deal with are substance abuse, domestic violence, single parenting, elder care, vocational rehabilitation, and mental disorders (NASW, 1993a).

Medical Settings

Clinical social workers are employed in acute care hospitals, emergency rooms, ambulatory care units, dialysis centers, and the like. Practitioners educate patients and their families about their illnesses, treatments, and surgical procedures they might anticipate. During the course of social work intervention, they help patients understand and cope with the psychological impact of illness. At times, they are called on to help the family accept that an organic etiology for the problem cannot be found—in other words, that the problem is psychogenic (Bergman, Contro, & Zivetz, 1984). They also help patients overcome obstacles to recovery.

Discharge and aftercare planning is one of the primary roles of medical social workers. They are generally seen as valuable members of interdisciplinary teams in hospital settings, often educating their teams about the psychosocial aspects of illness.

Acute Psychiatric Settings

Clinical social workers in psychiatric hospitals or psychiatric units of general hospitals share similar functions. They conduct high-risk evaluations and psychosocial assessments. During the patient's stay in the hospital, they educate and support the patient and family, often assuming the advocate role. They provide individual, family, and group therapy as well as crisis intervention. Again, they are valuable members of interdisciplinary teams. Discharge planning and aftercare planning are important aspects of their job (NASW, 1990).

Child Protection Services

Social workers investigate reports of neglected or abused children. Where necessary, they may initiate legal action to remove children from their homes, placing them in foster homes or temporary shelters until it is safe for them to be reunited with their families. They also provide direct services to children and families (e.g., therapy groups for incest victims, or parent-training classes). Child protection services are part of the child welfare system. Other settings within the public and private child welfare system include adoption agencies, foster care agencies, and family preservation agencies.

Family Service Agencies

Many family service centers were started by social workers. The mission is usually the preservation and welfare of the family. The range of problems that are seen concern the family's financial, vocational, medical, health, and mental health well-being. Workers counsel couples, families, and individuals. They might work with difficult adolescent problems or marital problems. They respond to emergency situations such as fires, floods, and earthquakes (Hopke, 1990).

Community Mental Health Centers

In 1963 Congress passed the Mentally Retarded Facilities and Community Mental Health Center Construction Act. This act and later legislation mandated federal funding for the construction of local community mental health centers. The centers were to provide basic services that would maintain mentally ill and developmentally disabled people in the community in the least restrictive environment. Clinical social workers continue to work in these centers, providing case management services and therapeutic care to chronically severely mentally ill and mentally retarded clients. Services include crisis intervention and short-term treatment.

College Counseling Centers

Student psychological centers employ clinical social workers along with psychiatrists and psychologists. Students are counseled for relationship problems, depression, adjustment to college, sexual identity issues, family crises, academic pressures, and the like. The format is usually individual and group counseling and tends to be oriented to crisis intervention and short-term treatment.

Prisons

Social workers employed in prisons focus on rehabilitation. They provide drug and alcohol addiction treatment and prerelease counseling to assist in the transition from incarceration to life in the community.

Courts

Social workers are employed by the courts as expert witnesses, counselors in victim-services programs, and probation and parole officers.

As probation officers, they essentially help offenders who have received a second chance from the court (providing they stay out of further trouble). As parole officers, they work with those who have been released from prison on the premise that they will start fresh and overcome their previous problems. Probation and parole officers provide emotional support and assistance with job training, employment, and suitable housing (Hopke, 1990).

Police Departments

Social workers employed within police departments provide a wide range of services for law enforcement officers, including substance abuse treatment, domestic counseling, and trauma and critical incident treatment or services.

Drug and Alcohol Rehabilitation

Clinical social workers provide drug and alcohol addiction treatment to adolescents and adults in outpatient programs, inpatient hospitals (e.g., Veterans Administration hospitals, residential settings, and halfway houses).

Long-Term Care Settings

Long-term care (LTC) consists of an array of services (health, personal care, and social services) that are needed on a continuing basis to enable the frail elderly or people with developmental disabilities or chronic disabling illnesses to maintain physical, social, and psychological functioning. Traditionally, these services have been provided in institutions. In the last decade, however, there has been a great deal of activity designed to provide long-term care services in the home. Goals are to help the elderly "age in place" and to make it possible for physically or emotionally disabled adults and youngsters to remain in their family homes. Clinical social workers practice in many types of long-term care settings, including senior centers, adult day care, nursing homes, hospices, group homes, and home health programs (i.e., delivery of health care in the home).

The Home

In the early days of the Charity Organization Society movement (the precursor to modern social work), home visiting was common practice. Paid agents visited homes to investigate applications and to determine the most appropriate intervention. They also applied "moral uplift" to improve the client's situation. After the early 1900s, home visits fell out of favor. Part of the reason for this change was the shift in social work philosophy from holding the environment responsible for human problems to believing that psychodynamic factors were responsible (Hancock & Pelton, 1989). Nevertheless, in the

1990s, there is renewed interest in delivering social work
services in the frail or disabled client's home.

Social workers in child protective settings still must enter
homes to investigate abuse charges. These home visits are often
difficult and dangerous (see Chapter 9 for a discussion about
keeping oneself safe while performing social work duties). The
literature on home visits commonly points out the difficulty of
the conflicting roles of investigating and helping. One successful example of programs of work in the home is the Homebuilders
Program (Gladow & Pecora, 1992), in which practitioners work
intensely (in the home) to decrease crisis and prevent family
dissolution. They spend 40 hours a week in the home and carry
beepers at night to remain on call for troubled families 24 hours
a day.

4

THE CLIENT

THERAPEUTIC CONFIGURATIONS

The major portion of this book addresses the treatment of individuals. The emphasis is on assessment, intervention, and the perplexing and sensitive questions that arise in *one-to-one* practice. Although social workers utilize other therapeutic configurations (such as couple, family, and group), one-to-one intervention remains the hallmark of direct practice.

Often individual treatment occurs because the social worker has no other choice. The client may not have any family, or family members may be too ill or live too far away to participate in the treatment. In other situations, family members are available, but one-to-one treatment remains the treatment of choice because of the nature of the complaints. However, when we make the shift from conceptualizing problems as exclusively individually determined to thinking of them as being affected and maintained by others, we are shifting into systemic treatment.

It is not uncommon for a social worker to use several different therapeutic configurations sequentially or alternately on the same case. For example, some years ago I treated a family consisting of Michael, an 8-year-old boy, and Paul, the single father who was raising him. Michael's parents had divorced two years earlier, and his mother rarely saw him. The presenting problems were Michael's behavioral difficulties at school and at home and Paul's ineffectiveness in controlling his son's behavior. Father and son lived a rather insular family life with no outside supports.

Throughout the helping process, Paul was seen individually to work on issues that affected his capacity to father Michael—for example, lingering grief about the divorce, loneliness, feelings of low self-worth, and other depressive features. Michael was also seen individually to help him resolve feelings about the divorce and about the mother who abandoned him. In conjoint sessions, Paul and Michael were helped to understand one another's emotional life and improve communication between them. Together they constructed guidelines for Michael's behavior and the consequences for infractions. Near the end of the helping process, Paul joined a support group for separated and divorced parents. In this group, he worked on parenting issues, dating, and his relationship with his ex-wife. The seasoned clinician must be able to move easily from working individually to systemically and back again.[1]

The issues discussed below are usually addressed in individual, couple, or group format. In practice, there is considerable overlap. For example, an incest victim may be seen individually, in group, or in family therapy. The choice would depend on a number of variables, including age of the client, when the incident(s) occurred, therapeutic goals, accessibility of family members, court mandate, and so forth.

Individual

Life Span Issues

Many periods during the course of life require decision-making and action—for instance, what job or career to pursue, with whom and when to make a relationship commitment, when to retire. Individuals may seek help in clarifying their goals and

---

[1]Griffin (1993) has written a basic primer on family therapy. Additional readings about the systemic perspective are under the heading "Couples and Families" in Appendix A.

values, resolving their internal conflicts, and diminishing the stress that emerges at these points.

Developmental Issues

Developmental crises may be even more compelling and stressful than life span issues. An example might be the young adult in the process of psychologically individuating and physically separating from his or her family. For those who are vulnerable, the stress of this period may precipitate an emotional or mental breakdown requiring mental health intervention. Sexual identity is another example of a developmental issue.

Adjustment Reactions

New situations and conditions, positive as well as negative, may overwhelm an individual's usual coping capacities. These might include diagnosis of a chronic or disabling disease, an unwanted pregnancy, being a victim of a violent crime, becoming homeless, separation, marriage, relocation, becoming a step parent (or getting one), age-related physical changes, and losses of any kind. Even winning the lottery might result in a crisis in coping for some individuals.

Personality Features

Clients who suffer from shyness, suspiciousness, lack of assertiveness, low self-worth, or poor self-image, for instance, may need to work individually before they feel comfortable in a therapeutic group.

Mental Disorders

Certain mental disorders such as phobias, obsessions, and post-traumatic stress respond well to individual treatment but may also require family intervention because of the effect that the disorder may have on family functioning.

Mourning

Both individual and group modalities are effective with grief work.

Couples

Poor Communication

One of the most frequently reported complaints by couples is poor communication. What this usually means is that one or both partners feel misunderstood, ignored, or denigrated by the other. Conflict erupts and results in hurt feelings and anger rather than resolution, satisfaction, or a renewed sense of intimacy. The ability to mutually problem solve and communicate is essential to resolving normal dilemmas, including the allocation of family resources and the way in which each mate relates to the other's family and friends.

Clinicians spend years perfecting their own communication skills. Thus, they are well suited to teach these skills to clients. Partners can be sensitized to the impact of their communications on their mates. They can learn to clarify their messages and practice giving and asking for feedback to avoid mistaken interpretations and misconceptions.

Sexual Dysfunction

Sexual dysfunction is a complex issue that may involve medical factors, psychological factors, and relationship issues. Assessment and intervention is likely to include collaboration with a physician. Apart from a purely functional disorder, treatment is probably best handled in couples' sessions.

Prenuptial Counseling

Issues may range from clarifying marital roles to mediating religious, racial, cultural, or value differences that impact the relationship. Counseling is preventive rather than curative.

Marital and Couple Life-Cycle Changes

Like individuals, couples pass through predictable life-cycle changes. Some milestones are traversed with little notice, whereas others are fraught with conflict, emotional upheaval, and temporary discomfort or confusion. The following are examples of common life-cycle changes in couples.[2]

---

[2]This text does not assume that couples are of the opposite gender. Where possible, reference has also been made to same-sex couples.

- Adjustment to a committed relationship or to marriage
- Family planning
- Adjusting to raising a child
- Last child leaving home (the "empty nest syndrome")
- Caring for aging parents
- Age-related changes in health, stamina, strength, and appearance (e.g., the "mid-life crisis")
- Disability or functional impairment of one or both partners

Infidelity

Exposure or suspicion of unfaithfulness often brings a couple to counseling. However, the partners may not have the same goals. One may want to work on reestablishing the sanctity of the relationship, while the other may want to leave the relationship and may be counting on the social worker to take care of the emotional distress of the abandoned partner. Infidelities occur for all sorts of reasons. They may signify a troubled relationship, an attempt at restoring individual self-esteem, an expression of anger, the search for a cure for boredom, or a sexual addiction.

Separation and Divorce Counseling or Mediation

Once the partners come to terms with the fact that the separation or divorce will occur, the formal "divorcing process" is set in motion. Numerous decisions and negotiations concerning child custody, property settlement, child visitation, and the like have to be finalized. Litigation, lawyers, and court costs tend to escalate the adversarial nature of the relationship. Some clinical social workers have taken on the daunting task of conducting mediation for couples who are ending their relationship. The assumption is that such mediation will keep the relationship amiable, keep the negotiations fair, and reduce the potential for costly legal fees.

One Symptomatic Partner

Woods and Hollis (1990) make the distinction between "acting-in" and "acting-out" symptoms (p. 383) of couples and how the symptoms affect the therapeutic configuration. Partners with acting-in symptoms turn their energy against themselves. They experience depressive symptoms, anxiety attacks, phobias, and the like. They tend to be the ones to seek individual treatment for their difficulties. Often, when invited, their partners will participate in conjoint sessions.

On the other hand, acting-out clients express rage and tend to engage in destructive or abusive behavior toward others. Rarely seeking treatment on their own, they are more likely to be coerced into treatment by their partners, spouses, employers, or outside social agencies (Woods & Hollis, 1990). Symptomatic persons may resist couples' sessions because they assume that they will be blamed by their partners for their behavior. In cases of abuse, the victim may likewise resist couples' work because of fear of further violence.

Religious, Racial, or Cultural Differences

Living with another person can be trying in the best of circumstances. Add cultural differences to the common difficulties experienced by couples and things can heat up.

The throes of romantic love seem to override such challenges in the early days of intermarriage or "intercoupling." That phase does not last forever, and conflicts tend to emerge and reemerge at various points along the lifecycle of the couple. Unable to resolve them together, couples will often seek help from a variety of sources, including family, friends, and clergy. Social workers and other professionals usually do not see these couples until things have deteriorated to the point of separation or until one of the partners has become symptomatic.

Family

When the goal is to improve the welfare of the family through intervention with family members, we may call that "social work with families." When the social worker meets with most or all members of the nuclear family, we can say that the "therapeutic configuration is family." When the clinician uses a theoretical framework in which the family is conceptualized as a single-client unit (or a system), we call that a "family therapy approach."[3] These terms are not mutually exclusive—that is, one can do "social work with families," seeing all the members of the family for the purpose of improving the welfare of the entire family unit. One can also use a family therapy approach with only one member of the family (Bowen, 1978).

Common family problems include the following:

- Family lifecycle issues (e.g., the birth of a new child, rivalry between siblings, an adult returning to school for a new career or job retraining)[4]
- Symptomatic family member (children are the most common identified patients)
- Divorce, remarriage, step-families
- Incest
- Disability or illness of a family member
- Caregiving obligations
- Parenting (parent–child discord or parental conflict over child rearing)
- Environmental stress (unemployment, poor housing conditions, poor health care, discrimination, dangerous neighborhood)
- Family violence

---

[3]There are a number of different family therapy models. Commonalities of the theories and practice of the various approaches include identifying the entire family as the client, an emphasis on the interaction between family members, and a focus on present behavior (rather than past behavior and family history). The techniques involve active participation and interaction between family members (e.g., role-playing, homework assignments) rather than the evoking of unconscious material or insight.

[4]It should be pointed out that there has been little research or literature on the gay and lesbian family cycle. One important difference is the general absence of traditional family rituals that mark the progression of the heterosexual family lifecycle, such as weddings and anniversaries (Slater & Mencher, 1991).

Group

The goal of group work, as in other therapeutic models or configurations, is *change*. The typical social work group consists of a clinician (sometimes two) who leads or facilitates the therapeutic interaction of a group of clients—usually 8 to 10. Rothman and Papell (1988) captured the essence of the group as a therapeutic method:

> The power of the group to effect change lies in its capacity to harness motivation and social need and to take action beyond that which any individual can undertake alone. Within the small group lies the potential for mutual aid, which supports and furthers the ideal of a humanistic social order in which people help each other rather than compete with each other. In the group, the individual can become socialized to humanistic norms. (p. 150)

Clients who participate in groups benefit from the support of others, the feeling that they are not alone in their problems and distress, and a sense of belonging and camaraderie. This format provides an opportunity to try out new behaviors, to learn from others, and to offer help in return. Social work groups are designed for the following purposes:

- Recreation
- Skill building
- Education
- Therapy
- Personal growth
- Socialization
- Self-help
- Support

Although groups are defined by their main purpose (e.g., socialization), members profit in a number of ways. For example, a mentally retarded young adult who attends a *socializa-*

tion group at the local community mental health center increases his interpersonal *skills*, learns from other group members about other activities he may enjoy around the city, considers the group fun (i.e., *recreational*), and on occasion is given a great deal of empathy for his daily frustrations and receives *support* for his efforts to live a full and rich life.

WORKING WITH DIFFERENCES

Clients present extraordinary variation. Some have had privileged childhoods; others have lived below the poverty level. A client could be a developmentally impaired 2-year-old or an octogenarian with dementia. A client might be a Native American adolescent living on a reservation, a second-generation Vietnamese immigrant, or an elderly Holocaust victim.

Race and Ethnicity

One cannot begin to make an accurate assessment or an effective intervention without first understanding a client's frame of reference. For instance, there is a tremendous variety in what individuals perceive to be problems or symptoms, their view of causality and the best way to "fix it" (or accept it), and their relationship with a "healer." In many cases, these perceptions are rooted in cultural values, beliefs, and traditions.

"Working with diversity" has been a pervasive theme in social work education for the last decade. Textbooks and papers have been written that emphasize differences in particular groups (e.g., McGoldrick et al., 1982; Red Horse, 1980; Sue & Sue, 1990). Other works seek to dispel racial and ethnic stereotypes and highlight intragroup heterogeneity (Gelfand & Fandetti, 1986; Ho, 1987) or focus on the commonalities among groups. Still others concentrate on helping clinicians become aware of their own values so that, despite differences between themselves and their clients, they may act in freedom from their own biases (e.g., Boyd-Franklin, 1989).

Clinicians must also have a racial and ethnic historical

understanding—that is, be cognizant of the way in which a particular group has been treated by the dominant culture as well as how it is currently being treated. They must also understand the group's patterns of adjustment to prejudice, discrimination, and oppression.

Lest we forget to acknowledge that even within groups there is great variation, Sue and Sue (1990) have developed a model to help clinicians understand *cultural identity development*. The model consists of five stages, each illustrating the way individuals struggle to understand themselves in relation to their own culture, the dominant culture, and the oppressive relationship between the two cultures. For example, in the first stage, individuals have an unequivocal preference for *dominant* cultural values, whereas in the fifth stage they have developed a sense of security and pride that allows them to appreciate the uniqueness of their own culture as well as that of the dominant culture. Knowing a client's stage of cultural identity development helps the clinical social worker understand the client's attitudes and beliefs.

Gender

Few dispute that there are obvious differences between the sexes—in cognition, emotion, and behavior. What is disputed is whether gender differences are primarily biological (genes, hormones, etc.) or are caused by personality differences rooted in anatomy (see, e.g., Wright, 1994). Other arguments suggest that the differences are a result of socialization. Still another perspective holds economic and political conditions responsible for what are considered appropriate gender roles and gender behavior. More than likely, gender differences are the result of an interaction of all of these factors. The bottom line is that the clinician must be aware of the influence of gender on what is labeled as a problem and in the way in which gender impacts treatment. For example, feminist therapy was founded on the notion that women (as well as men) suffer psychological and social problems because of sex-role stereotyping and sex discrimination. (For a discussion of feminist therapy and social work, see Van Der Bergh and Cooper, 1987.)

Immigrant Status

The migration experience has positive as well as negative implications for immigrants and their families. Clinicians need to be aware of the following:

- The drama and the trauma of the journey to the new land (e.g., flight under dangerous circumstances)
- The element of choice (i.e., those who are forced to migrate are more likely to have problems in adaptation than those who elect to migrate [see, e.g., Landau-Stanton, 1990])
- The rationale for migration (e.g., fleeing political persecution, pursuing medical help for a child, or seeking a better way of life)
- Expectations and disappointments
- Mourning for what was left behind
- The level of support in the new home
- Ways in which the family or individual has had to adapt to the new home (e.g., change in gender roles)
- The level of coping strategies (e.g., managing the conflicting values, traditions, and practices of two different cultures)
- The level of acculturation
- The relationship between the generations (e.g., the children acculturating more rapidly than their parents, contributing to stress within the family unit)
- The relationship of new immigrants to those in the community who immigrated earlier (e.g., membership in ethnic organizations and social groups; see Sluzki, 1979)

Geography

Where people live influences their perceptions of problems and treatment. For example, an elderly rural farm couple may view a proposed assessment by a geriatric team from a hospital in the nearest town as an interference (or threat) from outsiders. The clinician needs to consider that many people in rural communities are characterized by the following (outlined in Jennings, 1990):

- Trust and friendliness among community members
- Suspicion toward outsiders
- Reliance on friends, family, and neighbors for support
- Geographical isolation
- Resistance to change
- Independent spirit
- Financial and experiential poverty
- Concrete thinking and reserved behaviors
- Traditional values and conservatism

Although we sometimes think of the urban dweller as "open" to change and flexible in life-style, that is not the norm. Socio-economic class is a strong influence, as are cultural and ethnic traditions. For instance, in the midst of sophisticated, cosmopolitan urban areas, there are often homogeneous ethnic communities that may be quite insular, creating their own businesses, schools, and social groups, and holding fast to their ethnic values and traditions (Gelfand & Fandetti, 1986).

Sexual Orientation

Ten percent of the population live in a world in which whom they love and how they love present them with daily problems and challenges. Gay men and lesbians must cope with heterosexism (the pervasive belief that heterosexuality is the only "normal" manifestation of sexuality and that the heterosexual life-style is the superior and more valued life-style). They must also cope with homophobia (the prejudice, discrimination, disgust, avoidance, and hostility directed toward gay men and lesbians).

Gay men and lesbians have unique developmental crises such as the "coming out" experience. Partners are confronted with rules and regulations written with a heterosexist bias (e.g., few providers award health benefits to homosexual partners), and same-sex partners are not given legal rights to the personal effects or the body of their partner upon death. Child custody is still problematic. Despite these hardships, there is no evidence that gay men and lesbians have any more emotional problems than do people in the larger population (Dorfman et al., 1995).

Heterosexual clinical social workers must be informed about issues particular to the homosexual life experience. They must also be aware of community resources and especially aware of any heterosexual biases and homophobia of their own.

Disability

Physically, mentally, or developmentally disabled children and adults often have skill deficits that can be remediated with clinical techniques such as assertiveness training, communication skills training, problem solving, anger management, and so on. Intervention might also include teaching independent living skills (e.g., shopping, using public transportation).

When confronted with disability of any type, the practitioner needs to assess the impact of the disability on the client's self-image and sense of self-worth. The tendency is to conceptualize adjustment to disability as though it were static. For example, one may say that a child with a spinal injury has adjusted well to the permanency of a wheelchair. That may be so at the time. However, when the child reaches adolescence or young adulthood, there is likely to be a resurfacing of turmoil and a period of readjustment. Because the client appears to have adjusted to limitations, the social worker cannot assume that the disability will no longer be an issue.

Similar statements can be made for the family of the disabled client—that is, their adjustment is cyclic and ongoing. As with all of the differences we have discussed in this chapter, the clinician must be cognizant of the client's personal experience and the way in which discrimination and prejudice affect the client's well-being.

5

THE INITIAL INTERVIEW: ASSESSMENT

TO LOOK OR NOT TO LOOK: PREVIEWING THE CLIENT RECORD

The clinical social worker is informed about potential clients in many ways. In family service settings, for example, new cases may be presented at meetings at which workers volunteer to add them to their caseloads. In other settings, case assignments may be decided by a "case staffing team" of senior clinicians. At best, assignments are based on the fit between social worker expertise and client need, ethnic and racial match, or satisfying the clients' requests about their worker's gender, sexual orientation, age, and the like. At worst, assignments are based on who can squeeze yet another client into an already bulging caseload.

In medical settings, the client–social worker relationship may begin with a referral. For example, Dr. Smith states that Mr. James is having difficulty coping with his disease; he is not adhering to medical instructions and is combative with medical staff. "Please," says the referring physician to the social worker, "go in and see what you can do." The referral may be initiated because of an awareness that psychosocial aspects are affecting the patient's recovery.

In other settings, an *intake* worker may take a detailed psychosocial history and write it up. This may be face-to-face at the agency or conducted on the phone, with the intake worker sitting in front of a computer keyboard. The format of the psychosocial interview may follow a traditional common social work psychosocial history, or it may consist of a format particular to the agency. It is not uncommon for the format to be structured by an external funding source—for example, the county mental health department. The psychosocial history is placed in a client record or chart that may include a diagnostic label (usually motivated by a third-party reimbursement source) and an intervention plan. In still other settings (e.g., crisis centers), there may be nothing more in a client's initial record than a "face sheet" listing demographic information.

On occasion, the clinical social worker assigned to treat the client may have no more than a name and phone number taken off an answering machine or written down by a receptionist. On the other hand, the worker might be given a thick file comprising years of interdisciplinary evaluations, progress notes, and summaries from previous courses of treatment, including hospitalizations. The latter is especially true in residential settings and with adults who have been in the social service system since childhood.

Some clinicians choose not to read these client records until after their initial interview with the client. Such a reading, they believe, tends to taint an otherwise objective initial meeting. Others feel that the more information they have prior to the first meeting, the more efficient and effective they will be. Ultimately, each practitioner needs to decide what is best for him or her. However, early in one's career, it is probably best to take advantage of any available record, since being well-informed tends to increase confidence (a rare commodity with new practitioners). Experienced clinicians may value written or verbal information from their colleagues, but they have learned to suspend judgment affirming or negating the information as they come to know their clients over time.

ALLEVIATING ANXIETY: THEIRS AND YOURS

The first few minutes of the initial interview are a "warm-up." The clinician "starts where the client is," attending to what is occupying the client's thoughts at the moment, holding other agenda items for later. (These may include fee structure, requirements of a court-mandated intervention, and issues of confidentiality.) For example, if a client witnesses a mugging on the way to the appointment, nothing can be accomplished until that distress is attended to.

If the client is an "involuntary," his or her hostility, sullenness, and displeasure at having been "forced" to go to counseling must be addressed. Fischer (1978) believes that there are few truly "voluntary" clients. "Aside from the obvious institutionalized and legally coerced client, most people come to the attention of professionals such as caseworkers under pressure from family, peers, employees, or the unwanted burdens of their own problems" (p. 13).

The social worker notes the client's emotional state and encourages a discussion of feelings regarding coercion. Until a client is allowed to ventilate angry feelings to a nondefensive, empathic worker, nothing therapeutic is likely to occur. Novices, overconcerned with collecting facts and writing up psychosocial histories, may "miss" the distress and anxiety of the client.

The remedy is the 10-minute warm-up, which consists of questions and comments that, although innocuous, demonstrate concern. For instance, "Did you have any trouble finding the office?" "Were you able to find parking close by?" "How were my directions?"

When the worker notes the client's distress, anxiety, or confusion about finding himself in a social service setting, the clinician might say something like this:

Often people are upset or nervous about seeing a social worker. It is very common to feel embarrassed or angry. Sometimes, people might even think that it means that they are somehow a failure if they are in this situation. I want to assure you that there is no need to feel bad. Most people need some help with problems at some point in their life. Actually, seeking help shows courage.

Social work is generally misperceived. Students discover this
when they tell their family and friends that they want to go to
social work school. The stereotype of a social worker pulling
children out of the arms of mothers or of "sticking their noses"
into people's lives with no intent other than to satisfy their own
curiosity is quite pervasive. As a result of such stereotypes,
clients may feel that something "terrible" will happen to them
if they see a social worker. Although it is possible that something not desired by the client may occur, it is not usual. One
instance might be in the case of the involuntary client mandated
to treatment by the court. In such situations, reports that can
impact clients' lives may be required by the court. An example
might be the client who fails to fulfill treatment requirements
and thus does not regain child custody.

Ideally, the warm-up period reduces anxiety and helps clients understand the helping process and the therapeutic relationship. Clients often tell their social workers, "When I first
came here, I was scared to death."

It is also typical for novice and seasoned clinicians alike to
experience a degree of anxiety themselves during the initial
interview. For example, the clinician trainee may be unnerved
because his or her work is being observed through a one-way
mirror. A tape recorder may be on—with a client's written
permission, of course. (Techniques commonly used to super-
vise and train clinical social workers include observing therapeutic sessions through one-way mirrors, reviewing audio- or
videotapes, critiquing case presentations, and analyzing exten-
sive process notes.)

THE PRESENTING PROBLEM

Whether given a client's detailed psychosocial history or nothing more than a potential client's name, the clinician needs to
address the presenting problem directly. The presenting problem may be formulated by someone other than the client.
Another worker, a parent, a spouse, a teacher, or the court may
decide that the individual has a problem and may define the

nature of that problem. Nevertheless, the clinical social worker always asks clients for their perspective on the presenting problem. For example, "What brings you here?" "How can I help you?" "Do you have any idea why your neighbor might be concerned about your children?"

It is important to capture and record the client's own words regarding the problem. This description can be very prophetic. Clinicians I have trained often report that despite detours along the way, they frequently can rely on the original statement of the problem to get them back on track. One troubled teen reported, "My problem is that my parents hate me." Goals were eventually formulated that focused on his substance abuse and academic failures. Months later, at a family meeting, it became clear that the family was indeed enraged at him and that until the anger was expressed and understood by all family members—and somehow diminished—little of long-lasting consequence could be accomplished. That is not to say that the parental anger was the "cause" of the problems. In fact, it has aspects of both cause and consequence. However, the teenager was correct in naming it first and foremost among his current problems.

ECLECTIC ASSESSMENT

Assessment is the sine qua non of clinical social work. Whereas members of other disciplines may focus on the biomedical or the psychological, clinical social work considers *every* aspect of individual functioning and its relationship to understanding and resolving human problems.

Clinical social work has long since expanded from a sociological focus to a holistic assessment focus in which every relevant aspect of a client's life is considered. This entails a review of the client's past history as well as current functioning and includes affective, behavioral, and cognitive components. It also includes an evaluation of the client's internal and external strengths, resources, and coping abilities that can be harnessed in the service of problem solving and growth. This broad-sweeping approach, which examines a multitude of variables that might impact a client's problem, allows the practitioner to view the complexity of the client's situation.

Social work assessment is commonly called psychosocial assessment. However, it is much more correct to say that clinical social workers conduct "eclectic" assessments. The information they seek satisfies questions emanating from more than one theoretical orientation. For example, questions may be behavioral (about symptom duration, frequency, and intensity), cognitive (about thoughts), or psychodynamic (about dreams and fantasies). The eclectic assessment leads to a spectrum of multiple interventions that may be implemented one at a time or, in some cases, simultaneously.

Wherever clinical social workers practice—in schools, medical settings, correctional settings, hospices, rehabilitation centers, child protective agencies—they conduct comprehensive assessments. Clinical social workers *include* rather than *exclude* extraneous variables. Although the goal for the development of clinical practice and for assessment is to be empirically based, this eclectic or holistic approach is contrary to the narrowing and specifying of tasks that is currently favored by contemporary research methodology. Meyer (1992) has written that the way to manage such complexity is to employ simple means. She says to think big and do small, pointing to the environmentalists who think globally but act locally. In assessment and intervention, this means that we need to capture as much of the complexity of the phenomenon as possible and then use rigorous methods to define a "slice" of it that reflects the whole. Intervention is directed at those slices in which change brings repercussions upon the entire complex situation (Meyer, 1992).

The process begins with questions aimed at identifying and clarifying the presenting problem (i.e., why the client is seeking help). In addition to information gathered by interview, assessment tools may be used. These are formal questionnaires or checklists that record information. Interpretation of the scores informs the clinician about the presence or level of specific symptoms. No single formal assessment tool is used by all practitioners across all settings. In fact, hundreds of these tools are available (see Fischer & Corcoran, 1994, a resource for assessment tools). The best ones are brief and easy to administer. For example, Fischer and Corcoran (1994) have compiled two volumes of *rapid assessment instruments* (RAIs) to measure change within specific problem areas. Most contain under 50 items, which means that they will take only minutes to complete. However, instruments alone cannot substitute for rigorous interviews and observation in which practitioners collect data about a complexity of variables, eventually categorizing, summarizing, and drawing inferences that lead to case conceptualization and intervention (Meyer, 1992).

How does one know what questions to ask? Clinical social work education is well-grounded in human behavior in the social environment, abnormal behavior, practice skills (interviewing and treatment techniques), and cultural competence (ethnic, racial, gender, sexual, and geographical difference). Field training may include work with special populations (e.g., HIV-positive men and women, juvenile offenders, abused children) and problems (e.g., mental illness, homelessness, discrimination). It is out of these academic and clinical experiences that the social worker learns what kind of data is necessary to understand the person-in-the-situation and how best to elicit that information.

Adeptly formulated questions reveal relevant past and present living situations and the quality of human relationships in the family, at the workplace, at school, in the larger society. They reveal the inner life, the hopes and aspirations, the "shameful secrets," the regrets.

Assessment has a logical structure in that certain responses stimulate other questions or additional series of questions that may lead to still more areas for inquiry. In essence, assessment is a path that when stimulated by various markers proceeds in new directions, often returning to earlier questions for clarification.

The assessment of Tim, an adolescent, took many turns. Tim dropped out of the diving team at school, where he was the star diver. He was failing in school and was barely speaking to his father (they used to be close) or his mother. Dad reported that

Tim had taken up with "a bad bunch of friends." During the assessment phase, the social worker uncovered that the family relocates every couple of years because of the father's job. This led to questions about Tim's adjustment to this life-style. Tim reported that the last city, a rural town in Texas, was "the best place I have ever lived." This line of questions eventually led to Tim's bitter recall that his dad promised that the previous move would be the last. He broke that promise in less than two years.

Dad believed that Tim's school performance, long hair, and discontinuation of competitive diving proved that Tim was lazy and destined for "trouble." Assessment in each of these areas illuminated the situation. Tim was mourning the loss of his friends and the first town he felt at home in. He quit the team because the cold water and newly issued nylon swimsuits resulted in erections that embarrassed him every time he got out of the pool for another dive. The new school was academically more rigorous than the last. Tim was not motivated to get remedial help and decided he would return to Texas when he turned 18. He was furious at his father for breaking his promise with no explanation or apology. He described his father as a "hypocrite." "He's the one," he said, "who is taking drugs."

Further assessment revealed that substance abuse was a family problem. Dad was an alcoholic. Tim was experimenting heavily with a variety of illegal drugs. Mother was covering for both of them. The substance abuse information was not spontaneously offered but was obtained through skillful unequivocal questioning that took place over time in the context of sessions in which the clinician showed herself to be genuine, caring, and empathic.

WHEN ANOTHER PROFESSIONAL
CONDUCTS THE ASSESSMENT

Assessment continues throughout the intervention phase of the helping process. Even when the social worker is given an assessment conducted by another professional, he or she begins by updating the record. Additional assessment questions are in order. For example: "What has happened since you first made contact with the agency?" "What has happened since you talked with the intake worker?" "Is there anything that you haven't been asked about that might be important or that you might like us to know?"

ORGANIZING THE ASSESSMENT DOCUMENT

Information must be organized and interpreted. Ultimately the psychosocial history provides the history of the problem as well as the psychological, biological, and social precursors, maintainers, and consequences of the problem. Relevant categories may be added—for instance, "gang involvement," "reaction to dialysis," "history of foster placement," "drug history," "mental status."

CATEGORIES FOR ORGANIZING INFORMATION

Demographic Data

This includes age, gender, race or ethnicity, socioeconomic class, and immigrant status/generation (e.g., third-generation Japanese-American). Physical appearance should be noted—for example, unusual or bizarre clothing, unclean or inappropriate for the weather. Behavior during the interview is recorded (e.g., fidgety, agitated, or calm). Observable behavior, affect, and moods (e.g., hypervigilance, tearfulness, depressed facial expression) should be recorded as well. I have always found it important to ask about obvious injuries, scars, disabilities, tics, and such. This is a particularly difficult area to ask about because most people are taught, as children, to ignore such things. However, this sort of inquiry can reveal significant data. I can recall a youngster and his mother who were referred to the school social worker because of behavior problems. At the end of a lengthy assessment interview, the clinician asked the mother, "I notice that your left eyelid seems to droop. Does it cause you any difficulty?" She replied that it did not. The worker then inquired about how the condition occurred. The mother, with some hesitation, told of being struck by her husband in the presence of the child six months earlier. Up to that point, family violence had not been suspected or considered.

Presenting Problem

This is a statement, in the client's own words, about the problem that initiated the contact. The problem is clarified in detail. Questions might include, "How often does this occur?" "How long has it been going on?" "How long does it last?" "How severe is it?" "In what way does it interfere with the rest of your daily life?" "What other problems does it cause for you?"

Precipitating Event

Most clients struggle with their difficulties for some time before seeking treatment. What happened to make them ask for help at this time as opposed to last week, or last month? Why now? Sometimes an additional stressor has emerged, overwhelming the coping capacities of the client, or a family member or employer has threatened divorce or dismissal if behavior is not changed.

Current Functioning

How well one performs at work, cares for a family, progresses in school, maintains health, or remains safe in a dangerous environment reflects individual strengths and weaknesses. Comparison of previous and current functioning reveals the severity of the current problem.

Living Arrangements

The type of housing and a description of those who share the household may reveal potential support as well as sources of stress.

History of Presenting Problem

Examples of useful questions are: "Is the problem new or has this ever happened before?" "What kind of treatment did you receive in the past?" "What have you tried so far?" "What do your friends and family say about this problem?" "What do they think is the cause?" "What do they think you should do?" "What has worked in the past?" "What has not worked?"

Family History

A comprehensive history includes names, ages, genders, and relationships of several generations of family members in the client's family.

Developmental History

Individuals (adults as well as children) traverse a number of developmental milestones or tasks. Families, as well, weave their way through normal but sometimes difficult stages in the family life cycle. The clinician is aware of normal developmental processes and applies that knowledge to the assessment phase. What may be perceived as a problem may be no more than a developmental stage. For instance, helping parents understand that torn jeans, an earring, and a scraggly beard are normal expressions of adolescent development defuses family tension and power struggles. By the same token, discovering that an infant is not able to demonstrate the usual motor abilities for its age alerts the clinician to a possible developmental delay and a referral for an evaluation.

Educational/Occupational History

Again, this information provides a sense of a client's current and past functioning as well as a way of learning about strengths and weaknesses. It may also provide a window to the client's socioeconomic class, thus supplying a more complete understanding of the context of the client's problems.

Cultural/Ethnic Factors

Beliefs and customs that are unknown or misunderstood by the clinical social worker may seriously affect the development of the client–social worker relationship and may impede the helping process. Even verbal expressions can be misunderstood. I can recall a young African-American teenager who reported that she "tore up" a box of donuts. I took that as an expression of anger and plunged ahead with questions to uncover the source of that anger. Both of us eventually had a good laugh when we realized that I was unfamiliar with a common African-American "street language" phrase that expressed how she devoured the donuts with great relish.

Additional Types of Information

Spiritual/religious factors, sexual orientation/sexual history, health history (including hospitalization for physical or mental illness), and criminal history are among the areas that may be appropriate for assessment. "Is there anything that you think I should know about?" is a useful question. It suggests that clients may know something about their problem (consciously or unconsciously) that will assist the assessment and the helping process and gives them the opportunity to share it. The most striking example I can think of is the middle-aged grandmother who had suffered from chronic depression most of her life. The assessment was comprehensive and extended over several sessions. When I asked, "Is there anything else that you think I should know about?" she stated, "Yes, my brother raped me when I was 13 and I never told anyone."

Clinical Impressions

Under this rubric the clinician summarizes, analyzes, and clarifies the data that are relevant to the problems that trouble the client. The practitioner combines this with his or her understanding of the unique features of the client (e.g., weaknesses and strengths, external support and resources, living situation) and then states his or her impressions of the overt and covert mechanisms that contribute to the problem—in other words, a *working hypothesis*. The clinical social worker may include a diagnostic labeling where required. This does not include a treatment plan, although there may be some suggestions here for the treatment plan.

CASE CONCEPTUALIZATION: FROM ASSESSMENT TO INTERVENTION

When the assessment phase works well, the experienced clinician quickly "grasps the heart of the patient's problem and uses this information effectively to guide and focus the treatment" (Persons, 1994, p. 33). This "heart of the problem" might be called the *case conceptualization* or *case formulation*. It encompasses a broad understanding of the client and contains a statement about the problems and the nature of the mechanisms that underlie the client's difficulties. The most important aspect of case conceptualization is that it is the bridge to choosing particular intervention strategies.

The following example demonstrates the link between case conceptualization and intervention. A woman reports to the local community mental health center that her neighbor, Agnes Shore, an 87-year-old widow, appears to be malnourished—at least 20 pounds less than her former robustness. She reports that Agnes has stopped chatting with her over the backyard fence and stays inside most of the time. The woman observes that Agnes's grandson is her only visitor, and that he appears to be of "rough character." She reports that he rides a motorcycle, wears leather, and is unshaven and unkempt. She fears that he is abusing her elderly neighbor.

Upon investigation, the clinical social worker finds out that indeed Agnes is quite thin and is intermittently disoriented. Although there is food in the house, Agnes reports that she does not cook or eat very much anymore. It is difficult to assess the situation because many of the symptoms that might indicate depression could also be attributed to malnutrition or physical abuse. Agnes has several purplish patches on her forearms, is lethargic, and has lost weight. The grandson provides no useful information. He says, "I look in on her now and then. Everything seems okay to me."

The clinical social worker has several choices. If she does indeed suspect abuse, she will report the case to Adult Protective Services to initiate an investigation of abuse (see "Elder Abuse," Chapter 9). She can refer Agnes to the adult mental health services at the community mental health center for psychiatric evaluation of depressive illness or she can refer her for a full medical-neurological workup to rule out multi-infarct (stroke) or Alzheimer's disease. Much depends on her working hypothesis—that is, whether she suspects that Agnes's poor condition is a result of the grandson's physical/emotional/financial abuse, or if she believes that the weight loss and lethargy are a result of depression, or if she suspects that a stroke or dementia has decreased Agnes's level of functioning so that she is unable to cook or otherwise prepare a meal for herself, or some combination of all three. Although this is a very simplified example, one can see how case conceptualization leads to the choice of therapeutic strategies as well as to areas for further assessment.

THE THERAPEUTIC CONTRACT

Sometimes the contact ends at this point. For example, a recently unemployed single mother seeks financial help, but the agency provides only counseling. An appropriate referral is offered. (Social work distinguishes itself from other helping professions—medicine, psychiatry, psychology, nursing—by its knowledge of and linkage with community resources, such as formal and informal networks of health and social services.) However, if the client matches the agency's eligibility requirements and her needs match the function and resources of the agency, a contract can be formulated. Clinical social work is not a mysterious process. As soon as possible, the client is informed about the helping process and her role in it. The working hypothesis (in layperson's terms), treatment options, and descriptions of the treatments are all shared with the client.

In certain settings (e.g., crisis or medical), clients may be seen, on average, one to six times. It is an error, however, to believe that such limitations prohibit therapeutic change. It merely means that the helping process is brief and the goals modest. Number and duration of treatment sessions are usually predetermined by agency mission, resources, and theoretical orientation. Nevertheless, these details must be discussed with the client, and choices must be offered wherever possible. For example, an incarcerated youth may be asked, "What time do you prefer to meet? Four o'clock or five? Tuesday or Wednesday?"

Rules about confidentiality are stated concisely and unequivocally. Some clinicians provide a written statement outlining the limits of confidentiality and containing other important information. This statement is signed by the client with copies for both the social worker and the client. The sample form reproduced in Exhibit 5.1 reflects the type of information offered and a presentation format.

Confidentiality is not maintained where there is a risk of suicide or danger that the client may harm others (see Chapter 9). Although these exceptions to confidentiality may inhibit clients from revealing information, that is not always the case. In fact, many practitioners have noted that clients continue to express suicidal and homicidal ideations even when they know that their communication is likely to result in actions to thwart their intentions. Clients have said that knowing that their social worker would act to protect them and others from violence helped them to maintain control of their impulses.

The helping process is described, along with the parts the client and the social worker will play in the process. For instance, the worker might say:

> Mrs. Doheny, I agree that it appears that you do need help with your depression. I am willing to help you do what you need to do so that you can return to work and enjoy your life once more. Making changes like the ones you desire will take a bit of time. These kinds of changes do not occur overnight. We shall meet weekly for at least the next six to eight weeks. Your role will be to do any assignments that

Client Information Statement

The following describes information for new clients who desire individual, couple, family, or group therapy services from me. Please read this information sheet carefully and feel free to discuss any questions you might have with me.

1. I am licensed in the State of _____ as a clinical social worker, License number_____.

2. I am licensed by law and equipped by training to use psychological methods and techniques in a professional relationship to assist a person or persons to acquire greater human effectiveness or to modify feelings, conditions, attitudes, and behaviors that are emotionally, intellectually, or socially ineffective or maladjustive.

3. As a nonmedical therapist, I do not prescribe medication.

4. Confidentiality: Information shared, *including that of minors*, is kept strictly confidential except when the following legal limitations apply:

   - When the client communicates threat of bodily injury to another or is suicidal.
   - When there is reasonable suspicion of child abuse or abuse to a dependent adult that has occurred or will occur.
   - When information is required by law or ordered by the court.

5. I receive regular professional consultation; neither your name nor any identifying information about you is revealed.

6. In order for therapy to proceed most effectively, unless otherwise indicated, I will meet with you once each week for 50 minutes. I expect that you will keep each appointment except in cases of illness. I will begin on time and end on time except in cases of emergency. Since under

normal conditions neither of us will cancel an appointment with one another, and with the understanding that it is optimum that we meet each week unless prior arrangements have been made, I do not charge for canceled appointments made up the same week.

7. I use a 24-hour-a-day answering service, which you can reach by dialing _____. I check with my service several times a day for messages, and in cases of emergency they will make every effort to reach me directly. When I will be out of town or otherwise unavailable, a colleague will cover for me by checking with the service and being reachable in case of emergency. I will make every effort to apprise you of such instances ahead of time.

8. My fee for individual, couple, and family therapy is $_____ per 50-minute session. If your health insurance provides benefits for outpatient mental health services, after coverage has been verified I will accept your insurance assignment as partial payment of the fee. In most cases, you will still be required to pay any portion of my fee not covered due to deductible, required copayment, or limit of insurance reimbursement due to maximum allowed charges. Payment of full fee or mutually agreed-upon copayment is expected at the time of each service.

9. I am delighted to welcome you as a client of my practice. I encourage you to ask me any questions that come up about the structure of our professional relationship.

I have read and understand the above.

Signature _____
Date _____

Exhibit 5.1. Sample of client information statement.

From *Professional Business Forms for the Mental Health Clinician*, 1993, Sacramento, CA: California Society for Clinical Social Work. Copyright © 1993 by California Society for Clinical Social Work. Adapted with permission.

are required and complete the logs we talked about. I will help you to learn about what kinds of thoughts contribute to your depression as well as what kinds of activities might hasten your recovery. I believe that with the two of us working as a team, you should begin to notice results before long.

Child clients often worry about having to take medicine, getting needles, or being taken away from their family. Adults may worry that the social worker is going to confirm that they are crazy. With such fears, it is no wonder that people are anxious and likely to withhold information. Sometimes, clients—especially uneducated ones or those from nonWestern cultures—may believe that the worker will tell them what to do. These clients wait patiently for direct advice and are confused and disappointed when it doesn't come. I once worked with an Israeli couple who had marital problems. They asked repeatedly, "What should we do?" After I explained that they would have to come to their own decisions, they voiced their surprise. They had expected that I would, in Talmudic tradition, prescribe appropriate behavior for man and wife and, like Solomon, provide the solution to their marital dysfunction.

THE BEGINNER'S LAMENT: CAN I DO IT?

At this point, students and beginners get concerned. They say, "These clients deserve better. I don't know anything! I'm new at this." Although that is true, supervisors with expertise make it possible for inexperienced workers to treat clients while they develop their skills. The closer the supervision, the more workable the situation. For example, very early in my career a client presented with agoraphobia—"fear of the marketplace." I knew little about the treatment of this disorder. My supervisor led me each step of the way. Supervision was so close that when I spoke to my client, it was the supervisor's voice I heard coming from my lips.

Clinical social workers are trained to self-reflect so as to be aware of their emotional vulnerabilities and to recognize the personal problems that could impede the helping process. Those with little self-awareness are in danger of allowing their personality features and weaknesses to influence their therapeutic work. For example, a social worker who survived an abusive relationship might encounter a female client in an abusive relationship. The practitioner's experience could hinder or help the therapeutic process. For instance, the worker's own experience may enable her to empathically engage the client in productive problem solving. On the other hand, if the worker is unaware that she has generalized her anger towards her ex-husband to all men, her lack of objectivity may hinder the client's problem-solving capacity and encourage "acting out."

A person is said to be acting out when expressing strong emotions through behavior rather than verbally. The behavioral expression tends to be destructive and maladaptive (e.g., putting one's fist through a wall or getting drunk rather than addressing the emotion, which has more potential for self-understanding and resolution.) One of the goals of supervision is to assist supervisees in recognizing ways in which their personal history may interfere with their work. When this occurs, referral to another practitioner is the most ethical and effective course.

GOAL SETTING

The initial assessment phase is complete. Information has been gathered and organized. The case has been conceptualized, and a working hypothesis has been developed and shared with the client. The clinical social worker determines that she has sufficient self-awareness, expertise, and/or supervision to assist the client. The client agrees that help is needed. A time is set. However, there is one more crucial task that must be accomplished before meaningful clinical social work can continue. The significance of that task is demonstrated in the following vignette:

A beginning clinical social worker reports to his supervisor,

"I met with Mrs. Green and conducted an assessment, wrote it up as I was taught. Mrs. Green has not missed a session. She seems to like me. We agreed on the problem and I initiated the appropriate interventions and yet I feel lost. I don't know where I'm going. Nothing is happening. Everything is the same."

Workers may have a pleasant time dialoguing with a client. Clients are often funny or interesting. They might tell fascinating tales or weave intricate webs of delusions. The clinician may join in with clever interpretations or intellectual discussions—but alas, nothing happens. This is a consequence of inadequate goal setting.

Goal setting is an art. One has to formulate goals that can be accomplished. Just as important, one has to have a way of measuring goals to determine if, in fact, those goals have been achieved. Three things make goals unworkable—(1) the goals are too vague, (2) the goals are too big, or (3) the goals are unmeasurable.

For example, a client presents her problem as chronic wife abuse. She shows up at a shelter for battered women. After the initial interview and admission to the shelter, the worker says, "Let's set some goals." The client responds, "I want to get out of my marriage." As stated, that is not a workable goal. It is too big in its current form. To be accomplished, it has to be broken down into subgoals. "Getting out" of a marriage might require obtaining a lawyer, securing employment or job training, locating a place to live, and finding adequate financial and emotional support.

Another example is a couple who want to regain custody of a child. This is also too large a goal to tackle. One needs to partialize, breaking it down into smaller workable goals. The parents may need to demonstrate sobriety, participate in a parenting course, and obtain a clean, safe living arrangement.

Faced with many subgoals, the clinician must prioritize—that is, decide which goal should be addressed first. Often it is best to begin with the easiest, ensuring early success, building confidence, and thus increasing self-esteem. In the case of the abused wife, the subgoal of obtaining employment can be broken down further into still smaller subgoals—occupational training, social skills training, practice interviewing, obtaining suitable work clothing. However, at times, other goals take precedence over easy ones because they are more pressing. The battered wife needs to first obtain medical attention and legal protection from her batterer before seeking employment.

Goals structure the helping process. For example, Mr. Kent says, "I want to make friends." Here again, the goal is too large and too vague, and measurement is not defined. The clinician must gather additional information before subgoals can be formulated, partialized, and prioritized. The wish "to make friends" needs clarification. "What is a friend?" "How would you know if you had a friend? "What are the risks involved in having a friend?" "What are the benefits?" "Have you ever had a friend?" "What happens when you try to develop a friendship?"

Let's say that Mr. Kent conceptualizes "friend" as someone who has similar interests and is willing to share hobby-related activities. Further exploration reveals that Mr. Kent often is fearful of approaching someone he likes because he is unsure of how to start a conversation. Now we have the beginning of some subgoals—learning appropriate ways to initiate conversations, finding out where people with similar interests and hobbies might be found. Mr. Kent reports feeling anxiety when he attempts to approach people. A subgoal would be to reduce his social anxiety. Chapter 6 will focus on the intervention choices that are the result of a working hypothesis and goal setting. In Mr. Kent's case, appropriate intervention strategies might include anticipatory rehearsals, relaxation training and systematic desensitization, assertiveness training, and group therapy for singles.

6

INTERVENTION

Technique sets free the artistry.

—B. Leikind, *The Physics of Ballet.*

In 1917, social work had only one theoretical and practice model—*social casework.*[1] In the early 1920s, social casework was joined by another model, *psychoanalysis.* The 1930s brought two more models, and the next two decades ushered in others. In the 1960s and 1970s, a plethora of models developed, including family systems, behavioral and cognitive, and many others associated with the "human potential movement" (e.g., *gestalt, transactional analysis, existential social work*). Theoretical and practice models continue to proliferate (e.g., *hypnotherapy, feminist therapy, solution-centered therapy,* and a number of brief-treatment models). Corsini (1981), for example, has listed 250 different systems of psychotherapy.

Social workers traditionally view new therapeutic paradigms with great curiosity, enthusiasm, and hope. Unfortunately, many of these practice models are disappointing because their effectiveness does not withstand empirical scrutiny.

---

[1] A *theoretical model* explains human behavior and the nature of problem development. A *practice model,* on the other hand, is a set of concepts and techniques utilized to bring about affective, cognitive, or behavioral change. A practice model may evolve in several ways: It may develop from a particular theory of human development and human behavior, it may develop from experimentation, or it may be the consequences of clinical experience or "practice wisdom."

ECLECTIC CLINICAL SOCIAL WORK

In the late 1990s, clinical social work is both technically and theoretically eclectic. In an earlier survey of 1,037 clinical social workers, 256 identified themselves as eclectic. Another 146, who did not check off "eclectic," reported that they used two or more theoretical orientations, indicating by definition that they were eclectic (Jayaratne, 1982). There is no indication that this trend has changed in recent years. Nevertheless, additional research is needed to update theoretical trends in clinical practice.

There is no *single* professionally sanctioned social work practice model that is suitable and effective for all psychological and social problems, complex or simple. Contemporary social work practice tends to be *technically* eclectic, encompassing interventions from a variety of paradigms. In addition, social workers *view* individuals and their problems through several theoretical lenses.

The eclectic social work clinician, however, does not choose techniques indiscriminately in a haphazard "hit or miss" manner. Fischer (1978) offers an excellent explanation of eclectic practice:

> Eclecticism refers to a commitment to being guided in practice by what works, a commitment that takes precedence over devotion to any theoretical orientation. Thus, the practitioner can be divorced from any theoretical orientation currently in vogue. But eclectic practice requires the ultimate in flexibility and open-mindedness on the part of practitioners. They cannot afford to become complacent and satisfied with any one approach or any one technique no matter how efficient and effective it appears to be at a given time. This is because the knowledge used at any point in time will almost inevitably change as new research invalidates old. Thus, eclectic practice requires a continuing critical evaluative stance by practitioners. (p. 325)

Although one practitioner might select and employ different techniques in his or her practice than those chosen by another eclectic social worker, their selections share common origins. Theories and techniques for eclectic clinical social work practice must be

- congruent with social work values, ethics, and principles;
- compatible with the theory of psychosocial assessment and intervention (i.e., they consider individual and environmental influences in problem formulation and resolution);
- supportive of the social worker and client relationship;
- empirically validated (unfortunately, research lags behind theoretical and technical development, so this is not always possible).

MAKING CHOICES:
HIDDEN AND NOT-SO-HIDDEN INFLUENCES

The affinity that clinicians have for particular theories and techniques may be understood as a consequence of several influences (Rosen, 1988).

- Students find it wise to master the model that was embraced and taught in their school.
- Field supervisors (entrenched in particular orientations) insist that *their* model be exclusively practiced by their supervisees.
- Clinicians, taken with the work of a charismatic figure, imitate and adopt the role model's style and technique.
- Clinical work is often modeled after the practitioner's own psychotherapy experiences.
- Social workers may pursue expertise in a particular psychotherapy system because it matches their ideology or personality traits, or because it is congenial to their personality strengths or limitations. For instance,

an individual who is extroverted and expressive may "click" with an experiential therapy like gestalt, whereas a more "cerebrally oriented" individual may be attracted to the cognitive therapies.

- Students are attracted to orientations that embrace their view of reality—comic, romantic, ironic, or tragic (Messer, 1986).

This chapter will not focus on specific theoretical orientations or combinations of those orientations; this has been accomplished elsewhere (Corsini & Wedding, 1989; Dorfman, 1988b; Norcross, 1986; Turner, 1986; Whittaker & Tracy, 1989). Instead, it will focus on a broad sampling of concepts and techniques (drawn from various models) that are commonly incorporated into eclectic social work practice.

The Therapeutic Relationship

The relationship between the worker and client is central to the helping process. Unlike friendship, it is not based on mutuality. Emotional support, services, gifts, and other intimacies are not exchanged. Although the client and worker may be partners in problem solving, the clinician alone is in charge of enhancing the therapeutic relationship. The clinical social worker creates a context in which change occurs (i.e., where the client feels accepted, cared for, safe, and respected). The social worker must radiate warmth, empathy, genuineness, and a sincere interest in the client's life situation (past, present, and future).

Social workers who inspire trust and who are perceived as selfless in their concern are in a position to increase the client's motivation and feelings of self-efficacy. The client must perceive the clinician's positive regard as unconditional and the relationship as nonthreatening. Individuals who choose to become clinical social workers usually possess some degree of these characteristics. However, merely possessing these qualities does not mean that one knows how to use them optimally for therapeutic advantage. That skill is honed in professional social work education.

Structure of the Helping Process

A well-thought-out plan and the systematic use of specific techniques to influence the problem provide the structure for the therapeutic process. In the broadest sense, the helping process has a beginning, a middle, and an ending phase. Each phase has specific tasks. The beginning includes building rapport with the client; conducting an assessment; setting goals; contracting for frequency, number, and duration of sessions; setting the fee; and explaining the helping process and worker and client roles. The middle phase emphasizes interventions (homework assignments; refining of goals; working through transference, countertransference, and resistance; and utilizing resources). The end phase includes evaluating outcome, resolving feelings about the end (termination) of the therapeutic relationship, and making arrangements for maintaining gains and monitoring ongoing services.

Content and Process

Because people communicate their thoughts and feelings through words, gestures, facial expressions, posture, voice tone and volume, dress, and behavior, clinicians constantly shift their attention from one vehicle of communication to another. A social worker who attends to only one form of communication (e.g., verbal) perceives valuable but incomplete information. The primary foci of attention are known as content and process.

Content consists of the words that are spoken by the client, whereas *process* is an abstract conceptualization of what is transpiring during a particular period of observation or interaction between the worker and the client. The process is deducted from information from multiple pathways of communication.

Content and process are best explained by an example. Janet and other members of her family have been court mandated for treatment following an investigation conducted by the Department of Children's Services that revealed Janet's history of sexual abuse (first as a victim of her father and older brother and later as her younger cousin's perpetrator).

Twelve-year-old Janet sits on a chair facing the social worker. It is the beginning phase of the helping process, and the worker is attempting to build rapport with his young client. Janet talks of school friends and favorite TV shows. Although the words, or content, of the communication are typical for any 12-year-old, the worker gradually becomes aware of his uneasiness and diverts his attention to the process of the session. Shifting his attention from her words to other avenues of communication, he realizes that Janet is expressing precocious sexuality via body posturing, flirtatious glances, and provocative tone, and is probably testing his response.

The Working Hypothesis

Assessment provides raw data, including personal and family history and information about current psychological and social functioning, environmental influences, and individual strengths and limitations. From this raw data, clinicians draw conclusions. They conceptualize the genesis of the problem(s) and speculate on the factors maintaining the problem and prohibiting resolution. This conceptualization is provisional and changes as a deeper understanding is gained over time. The following are examples of provisional conclusions or *working hypotheses*:

- The Greene family has become disorganized, chaotic, and overwhelmed as a result of Mr. Greene's unemployment and subsequent major depression, Mrs. Greene's physical illness, and deteriorating living conditions in their recently condemned apartment building. The oldest child's shoplifting represents a desperate effort to compensate for the loss of a stable and predictable family environment.

- Mr. Smith's difficulty in forming trusting relationships as an adult is related to a childhood marked by the instability of living in six foster homes and the physical abuse he suffered at the hands of several foster parents.

- Ms. Baker's fear of public speaking is related to a childhood trauma in which a teacher humiliated her in front of an auditorium full of peers.

- Mr. Granville's nonadherence to his medication regime is, in part, related to his efforts to regain control of his life as well as his belief in the nonmedical treatment of disease.

Working Through

It is a common phenomenon in clinical work for clients to repeat their "story" innumerable times. This is often referred to as *working through*. Session after session, the client feels compelled to relate, for instance, the same story of victimization, loss, or disappointment. The clinician provides support and therapeutic responses (varying the wording where he or she is able, so as not to get locked in a repetitive dialogue with the client).

I recall the case of a middle-aged woman whose husband deserted her for his secretary. The client repeatedly lamented the same story of unfairness, shock, and guilt (for "letting herself go").

The clinical social worker was technically competent, yet no change occurred. Eventually, the social worker began to question her own competence and her choice of profession. One day, the client came to the clinic at the appointed time, flaunting a new hairstyle and new hair color. She looked brighter and less depressed. She asked for help in learning to socialize more and reported instances of assertiveness with her sons and ex-husband the previous week. The social worker could not understand the change. She had tried no new techniques. Nothing of consequence had happened during the week to merit such a dramatic change.

This is a *magic number* phenomenon. It appears that, on occasion, clients need to repeat the facts and feelings around their dilemma for an indeterminate number of times. At the outset, the "magic number" is an unknown. It may be two or 200. The social worker can only "bear witness" and make appropriate therapeutic comments. When the magic number is reached, the work may end or move on to new areas for exploration and intervention. The magic number is particularly common in mourning. Ego psychology–oriented theory would posit that the client's ego is gradually adapting or coping to her situation, and thus the change is a reflection of emerging ego strength. Psychoanalytic theory would posit that the process of recounting the events of her situation signified that unconscious material had become conscious, resulting in restored mental health.

Self-Awareness of the Social Worker

Everyone has blind spots or "triggers" (areas of vulnerability) that, when stimulated, cause them to have strong emotional reactions. These triggers usually, but not always, are rooted in the past. Most people are only minimally aware of them. An example would be a woman whose childhood was marred by a dependent, hypochondriacal mother. In adulthood, the woman finds herself with little tolerance for complaints, and she tends to react with unusual hostility when people complain of physical symptoms. Another person, raised in a family where racial slurs are commonly expressed, finds himself uncomfortable when in close proximity to individuals from other racial backgrounds. In ordinary life, such lack of self-awareness (i.e., understanding the roots of one's feelings or actions) may or may not be troubling. However, in the practitioner, they may (at best) obstruct the delivery of quality clinical treatment and (at worst) endanger the well-being of the client.

Social work education emphasizes the development of self-awareness. During professional training, workers are constantly required to monitor their own feelings and actions to uncover blind spots and biases. Supervisors observe beginners at work and ask pointed questions during supervision to detect such blind spots and biases. Personal therapy for students is often recommended for this reason. Self-awareness is seen as necessary so that the therapeutic work with a client is uncontaminated by personal blind spots.

Self-Awareness of the Client

Clients, as well, are poorly served by their own biases and blind spots. Even in situations where clients have played no part in the problem formation, they participate to some degree in problem continuance or resolution. Unaware clients are in a "box," unable to observe themselves and thus unable to "see" how they work to maintain their problems. Social workers, outside the figurative box, help clients develop the capacity for self-observation and self-understanding (see Exhibit 6.1). The job of the clinical social worker is to comment on—or sometimes confront—clients' behavior and urge the clients to consider their contribution to unsatisfactory relationships or other problems in living. For example, clients may come to understand their motivations, desires, dysfunctional beliefs, defenses, and how they are perceived by others. The therapeutic process helps clients to develop the language and concepts to become self-aware, thus ultimately increasing their behavioral choices (an ideal that is rooted in the social work value system).

The Unconscious

The concept of the unconscious is the keystone of psychoanalytic theory. It is believed that an individual's problems are rooted in childhood trauma or repressed thoughts or impulses. In psychodynamic theories, improvement or cure of the client's symptoms is sought by restoring these memories, thoughts, or

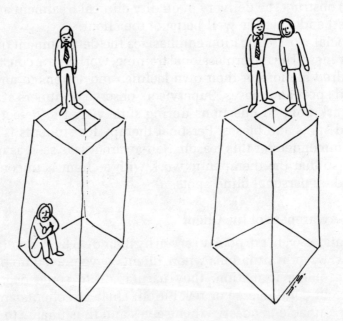

Exhibit 6.1. Helping the client develop self-observation.

impulses to consciousness. In other paradigms (e.g., family systems and behavioral), less attention is paid to unconscious phenomena, and more attention is focused on "here and now" behaviors and what to do to reinforce them.

Insight

When, through self-awareness and self-understanding, clients achieve knowledge about the origin of their difficulties and the way in which they and others have contributed to the current situation, they are said to have gained insight.

A useful technique to assist the client in gaining insight is the statement "I wonder" followed by a hypothesis regarding the client's difficulties, patterns of behavior, and so on (see Exhibit 6.2). For example, to an elderly man who has a problem with alcohol, the social worker might say, "I wonder if your increased drinking has anything to do with your wife's illness?" To an adolescent with uneven performance in high school, "I wonder if how well you do in your classes has anything to do with your feelings about specific teachers?" To an unwed mother of 15, "I wonder if wanting a baby had anything to do with your situation at home?"

Coping Mechanisms

Problems activate coping efforts. An optimistic view of people, derived from ego psychology, is that with help they can resolve their own problems with behaviors that are used to adjust to or adapt to internal or external stressors.

Mr. White is very aware of time and hates to waste it with meaningless activity. To do so usually makes him feel anxious and unhappy, so he has developed a number of coping mechanisms. For example, he knows that a visit to the dentist will involve a half hour in the waiting room. He takes care of himself by bringing his checkbook and monthly statement or some correspondence with him. The time spent waiting is used to balance his checkbook or write letters so he needn't be annoyed about wasting time.

Exhibit 6.2. The "I wonder" technique for stimulating insight.

Strengths/Limitations

When an individual identifies problems and seeks help to resolve those difficulties, the tendency among lay people and professionals alike is to focus on weaknesses—that is, the flaws, deficits, and impairments that contributed to the problems in the first place and that interfere with the ability to overcome them. Clinical social work, however, focuses instead on uncovering a client's strengths and utilizing them for problem solving. Strengths that can be brought to bear on the client's difficulties include intelligence, persistence, courage, creativity, energy, integrity, patience, interpersonal skills, leadership qualities, and talents of many sorts. It is often these strengths that have helped individuals survive as well as they have in the face of considerable hardship.

Supervision

In practically every setting in which you find social workers, there is an administrative and educational supervision function. Typically, supervisors are seasoned professionals who help the social workers refine their clinical skills and understand and implement agency policy. We sometimes note a "parallel process" in supervision and in the helping process. While the social worker is helping clients expand their flexibility and life choices, increase their problem-solving skills, and accomplish their goals within a trusting, nonjudgmental, accepting, supportive relationship, the supervisor is helping the supervisee increase his or her skills and accomplish goals within a trusting, nonjudgmental, accepting, supportive relationship.

Resistance

Traditionally, the psychoanalytic term "resistance" referred to anything in the client's behavior (e.g., holding back information, changing the subject, or other methods of disengaging from the therapeutic process) that interrupted the progress of the analytic work. Resistance was expected and understood as benign and largely out of the client's control. More recently, those in the helping professions have used it to "blame the victim," attributing it to clients who are unmotivated or unwilling to change (i.e., who manifest a deliberate refusal to cooperate with the helping process).

Contemporary clinical social work, on the other hand, sees resistance as a sign that the helping *process*, not the client, has broken down (Nelson, 1975). There is a feeling of being "stuck." The following are examples of resistance:

- The client communicates that he does not want to provide information (e.g., a teenage boy looks everywhere except at the worker; he shrugs his shoulders).

- The client is late or misses appointments (although this could also be for economic reasons, such as no bus fare or no child care).

- The client brings up issues clearly unrelated to the work (e.g., the weather).
- The client uses methods of defense to avoid anxiety-provoking material (e.g., intellectualization).
- The social worker avoids pertinent areas because she is not confident of her ability to handle certain subjects.

A number of problems may result in a breakdown of the helping process. Frequently, the social worker has not provided the client with adequate preparation for the therapeutic work or attended to the client's anxiety. The client may be confused about the nature of the therapeutic process and the client and social worker roles. The client may fear becoming overwhelmed by emotion or may be afraid that the worker will judge him or her negatively.

Addressing the resistance directly usually gets things moving again. The clinician does this by formulating a hypothesis about the origin of the resistance and then speaking frankly about it. For example, "It seems that whenever we talk about your marriage, the subject gets changed to your child's poor manners" or "Are you concerned about how I will use the information you might give to me?"

In some situations, simply drawing attention to the resistance resolves it. For example, when a client's tear-filled eyes betray efforts to hold back material, the question "Are you experiencing some emotion now?" usually opens the lock on the inhibited emotion, releasing a deluge of troubling thoughts and feelings. Directness is sometimes responded to with denial, but later—during the same session or the next one—the client articulates concern and work resumes.

Sometimes noting the "resistance" is enough to extinguish it. This is particularly true with teenagers. I worked with a 16-year-old whose favorite response seemed to be "I don't know." We had a warm relationship, and I was certain that he did not dislike me. Nevertheless, there were days when he would lapse into "I don't know," and I did not have the skill to resolve the impasse. Finally I addressed it head on, saying, "I notice that every time I approach a subject that you prefer to avoid, you say

'I don't know.' " He did not respond. The next time he said "I don't know" I said, "There it goes again, another 'I don't know.' We must be getting into a subject that you would rather avoid." After saying "I don't know" a few more times, the client began to laugh when he said it. The result was greater self-awareness for him, a less serious attitude for me, and a significantly diminished resistance.

Environmental Fit

Social work subscribes to the notion that individual well-being is dependent on how well features of the environment fit with an individual's characteristics and needs. The origins of this theory are in Lewin's (1951) notion that behavior is a function of the relationship between the person and the environment. Thus, clinical social workers consider the environment and the person and how well they fit together during the assessment phase as well as in the intervention phase of the helping process.

TECHNIQUES

Relationship Building

Consistent care and understanding are in themselves therapeutic; moreover, they set the stage for change. Active listening is an important aspect of that process. Active listening requires undivided attention. Clinicians demonstrate that they understand the client by occasionally paraphrasing what the client has just expressed. For example, "You seem to be saying that although you want to believe that your husband has changed, you still have serious doubts."

Imagery

The therapeutic process may be enhanced through the use of images. Imagery may be used for relaxation training. For instance, the clinician may create and guide the client through a fantasy that contains elements that are relaxing for most people (e.g., the beach, a pleasant walk in a favorite place). Simonton

(1978) used guided imagery to stimulate the body's capacity to fight cancer cells. It has been used to help clients "mentally prepare" for a host of difficult anticipated situations.

In assessment, the practitioner may ask the client to visualize a particular stressful situation, sharing the thoughts that come to mind. This is useful for uncovering dysfunctional cognitions that keep a client stuck and unable to make the necessary changes. Imagery-based techniques in behavior therapy have been well-established, particularly systematic desensitization. This technique is based on a simple premise: One cannot be anxious and relaxed at the same time (Wolpe, 1985). Clients are taught a method of progressive relaxation in which they system-atically relax different muscle groups. This produces a lower state of physical arousal and a feeling of relaxation or calmness. Prior to this training, the practitioner and the client construct a hierarchy of situations that normally induce a state of anxiety in the client. For example, for a client who has severe problems dealing with authority figures to the point that he becomes anxious and nearly incoherent when he must talk with his boss or meet with his child's school principal, the constructed hierarchy of situations might range from getting a letter from the school requesting a meeting with the principal, to actually entering the school building, to sitting in the principal's office discussing his daughter's behavior. In treatment, the client is asked to first become deeply relaxed using the method he was taught. Then he is asked to conjure up the least anxiety-provoking image on his list. If he feels no anxiety, he conjures up the next item. If, at any point, he feels anxious, he is asked to implement the relaxation technique. This is repeated until the client can remain calm and relaxed while visualizing each scene on the continuum. This method is particularly useful for the treatment of phobias.

When the social worker experiences a spontaneous image during a session, it makes good clinical sense to attend to it. For instance, if an image of a many-tiered parking lot pops up in the clinician's mind's eye, it may be no more than a temporary distraction, indicating that the social worker is focusing not on the client but on finding his car in the crowded parking garage after work.

On the other hand, clinicians' images may also provide important clues to the process level of the client–worker interaction. For example, I can recall visualizing a waiflike, smudged-faced, shabbily dressed little orphan girl while listening to my female client relate her life history. I realized then (and it was confirmed later) that my client, although quite bright and competent, was very invested in being perceived as a helpless victim. She was working overtime in her portrayal. I have often shared such images with clients, with good results (see Exhibit 6.3).

Directive Influences: Advice Giving and Education

Social workers have traditionally shied away from giving advice because it seems counter to the professional principle of client self-determination. However, the reality of practice is that sometimes guidance, in the form of advice, *is* appropriate. In common with any other intervention, it should be delivered skillfully, with a clear understanding of the ramifications.

Woods and Hollis (1990, pp. 111–112) describe four levels of directiveness:

- Underlining—Agreeing with a course of action that the client is already contemplating. For instance, the client states that he might be starting to hear voices again, and perhaps he should make an appointment with his psychiatrist. The worker nods her head in agreement.

- Suggestion—The worker conveys her inclination toward a course of action. However, it is delivered in such a way that the client may reject it without feeling that he is going against his worker's definite opinion. For example, the client reports hearing voices, and the worker states, "With your past history, it probably makes good sense to check in with your psychiatrist."

- Urging/Insisting—Giving advice with a degree of forcefulness. The client reports hearing voices, and the worker says, "It is essential for you to make an appointment immediately. You are in danger of having a serious breakdown and another hospitalization."

Exhibit 6.3. Images are important clues in understanding clients.

- Actual intervention in the client's life. This might take the form of a forceful intervention: The worker reacts to the client's report that the voices are commanding him to kill himself by initiating an involuntary commitment to a psychiatric hospital for evaluation. Or it might include invoking authority: "I am sorry, Mrs. White, but if you don't complete the parent-training process, I will have to report that to the court. Remember, the judge said that you would have to comply with *all* of the stipulations to have your children returned."

In general, clients should be encouraged to make their own decisions. However, a gentle suggestion or reinforcement of a client's conclusions is often helpful (Woods & Hollis, 1990). Direct advice is commonly given, especially in areas in which the worker clearly has expertise, such as child rearing or obtaining social service, welfare benefits, and entitlements.

Metaphors, Anecdotes, and Fables

I can remember the fairy tales I used to hear as a child and the question that I was often asked at the end of the story. "Do you know the moral to this story?" would send me into hard thinking, trying to unearth the secret of the fable (which was usually a lesson about good and evil or right and wrong). The therapeutic use of metaphors and anecdotes does not require the client to verbalize a "moral" or a lesson. Most times the client is not even aware that he has just heard a therapeutic metaphor or anecdote. The theory is that, via a fable or a story, the clinician is communicating directly with the client's unconscious. The message is absorbed by the unconscious, where it will then be incorporated and (we hope) used to improve the client's situation.

Metaphors appeal to the unconscious (Fox, 1989). The clinician selects a word or phrase that is familiar to the client because it is common to his or her job or hobby. However, the social worker uses the word to communicate the obvious as well as the covert therapeutic message. Perhaps the client is a gardener. In such a case, she (or her unconscious mind) might be more likely to respond to gardening metaphors than to the usual therapeutic suggestions. For example, "In the spring, Mrs. McDonald, you may decide that the time is right for new seeds to be planted. Of course, any new seeds need attention. They don't grow into their promise without proper nurturing and patience. Some good planning, time, and the right climate may bring you the harvest you dream of."

Sometimes metaphor is used as a shorthand way to emphasize points or as a special code between social worker and client. For example, a young woman once sought my services because she feared that constant fights with her boyfriend would result in a breakup. This was particularly stressful because they were to be married in a few months. I saw her individually and with her boyfriend. Among the many problems identified was that the woman was quite materialistic and always seemed to want more than she had. While we worked on the genesis of her lack of satisfaction, I needed to help her first get a sense that she was, in fact, making demands.

She wore a three-carat diamond engagement ring. Her fiancé bought a large home for them to live in. Her parents were giving her a lavish wedding and a luxurious honeymoon. After inspecting the new house, she complained that she couldn't possibly use the oven. It was not the "top of the line" model, and not the right shade of off-white to match the decor. She could not understand why her boyfriend refused to have it replaced and why he offered little sympathy for her distress. We had talked of her constant need to receive bigger and better things to feel better about herself. I used the oven as a prime example, restating that another perspective on her situation was that although she had a diamond ring, a new home, extravagant wedding arrangements, and a first-class honeymoon plan, she remained unhappy because of an oven. She was able to see, at least for the moment, the unreasonableness of her demands. Every time her unreasonable demands surfaced again, I merely said, "Whoa, that sounds like another oven." Thus the oven became a therapeutic metaphor for her materialism and the pain it caused her and those around her.

Self-Disclosure

The *Social Work Dictionary* (Barker, 1991) defines self-disclosure (also called therapist transparency) as the "worker's revelation of personal information, values, and behaviors to the client...There is some consensus that it should not occur unless it serves a therapeutic purpose or is designed to help achieve the client's goal" (p. 210).

I have learned many things from my clients, including factual information such as how one trains for weight-lifting competition or survives drugs and violence on inner-city streets. Also, one's clinical competence improves through the successes and failures experienced in practice. All of that, however, is a "perk," a fortunate by-product of the work. Although they may benefit by professional growth, social workers should not benefit personally (i.e., by sharing their own problems with clients). Disclosure of personal information to the client should occur only when it is part of a planned intervention.

An example from my own practice illustrates the therapeutic

use of self-disclosure. The client I was working with was a middle-aged single man. Although he desired a meaningful relationship with a woman, he had never had such a relationship. Among other problems, he was painfully self-conscious and suffered from low self-esteem. During the helping process he had been able to gain understanding about the childhood roots of his problem. We were working behaviorally to help him develop his social skills and increase his confidence. For several months, I watched him appear for our sessions at the family service agency appropriately dressed and eager to plunge into the work. However, he never removed his hat, a snappy number with a narrow brim. Finally it dawned on me that he must be bald. One day, I saw my opportunity. We were discussing the way in which one's beliefs contributed to one's feelings and ultimate behavior. I told him that I had a personal experience with how one of my own beliefs had affected my behavior. I disclosed to him that I had, I believed, ten of the ugliest toes to be found. Self-conscious about my feet for most of my life, I never wore open-toed sandals or exposed my feet unless I had absolutely no choice, such as at the beach. I also shared that after many observations of other (even uglier) feet shod in sandals and exposed boldly to me, I realized that my "ugly toes" were largely my own perception. Other women, with worse feet, enjoyed the coolness of sandals. What's more, no one else seemed at all disturbed or even noticed other people's feet. The result was that I fought against my maladaptive belief, bared my feet in the summer, and eventually forgot about my former embarrassment. We both laughed over my personal disclosure. The next week, my client appeared without his hat, with a lovely bald head, and with a grin on his face.

Processing

Clients (and clinicians) frequently get mired down in minute details, relaying names, places, precise times, and the like. Stopping to *process* by saying "What is really going on here at this moment?" can help the client by bringing maladaptive behaviors into awareness and creating an environment in which change can occur. For example, the client might respond, "I guess I am trying to avoid talking about upsetting things."

Interpretation

There is a very old cliché about "not being able to see the forest for the trees." People are often so immersed in their difficulties that they cannot "see" them clearly. They lack the benefit of a detached perspective. Their understanding of their own current situation or behavior and what contributed to it is marred by emotion, distorted views of reality, lack of information, and so on. However, it is always best for clients to come to these kinds of understandings themselves. The experience of "putting the pieces together" oneself is very powerful. For instance, a chronically unemployed man said, "You know, sometimes I think that I argue with whoever happens to be my boss because I am still trying to 'one-up' my father." There are times when clients need this kind of insight but are unable to gain it on their own. *Interpretation* is an intervention in which the clinician decides that it is more expedient or appropriate to not wait for spontaneous insight but to offer such explanations for the clients to consider.

Contracting

In the current climate of managed care and limited federal, state, and county funding for social services, calls for accountability and demand for brief forms of treatment are the norm. Clinical social work treatment is rarely open-ended and without specific goals. The problems to be worked on and in what order (although working on one may have effects on others), the methods of reaching goals, and clinician and client tasks are nearly always agreed on verbally or in a written contract.

A "suicide contract" is another type of therapeutic agreement that may be employed (Corey, Corey, & Callanan, 1993). The clinician seeks client agreement that he or she will call on a specified contact (a family member, a hot line, or a professional) if suicidal feelings emerge. Sometimes the contract will be that the client promises not to attempt suicide during a specified period.

Role-Playing

Every child who pretends to be a rock star or an astronaut or who imitates Mommy and Daddy is role-playing. Although there are many of us who still role-play rock stars or supermodels in our underwear, in front of the mirror in the privacy of our own bedrooms, this form of play has for the most part faded by adulthood.

The therapeutic use of role-playing is said to have been initiated by J. L. Moreno in his psychodrama method (Moreno, 1970). However, it is a technique shared by many therapies, including family, behavioral, gestalt, cognitive, and group. Clinical social workers use it for a number of purposes:

- Behavioral rehearsal of anticipated events (e.g., asking for a raise)
- Assessment (e.g., a couple reenacts an argument, thereby demonstrating their skills or lack of skills in resolving marital conflict)
- Gaining understanding of other's experience (e.g., a mother role-playing her ill child)
- Developing new skills (e.g., assertiveness)
- Developing self-awareness (e.g., identifying thoughts or emotions that arise in certain situations)
- Clarifying internal conflict (e.g., the client acts the part of the self that wants to leave the marriage and the part of the self that wants to stay)

Clarification

Clarification is a technique that is rooted in psychoanalytic thought (Woods & Hollis, 1990). The social worker paraphrases or reflects the client's statements (e.g., "You say you want to be a good mother, but no one will let you?") to help clients separate their distortions of external events from objective reality. It is an educational technique as well as a therapeutic one. An example of the latter is *values clarification*, a process in which individuals are assisted in examining their personal beliefs and ideals and the relationship of those values to their behavior.

Modeling

Learning through imitation and observation of others is associated with behavior therapy. However, the method of modeling desirable behavior for clients has a long social work history. The friendly visitors of the early 1900s would "by their example, attempt to guide families out of poverty and suffering" (Dorfman, 1988a, p.6).

Contemporary social workers are well aware of the therapeutic potential of vicarious learning. They will often model parenting skills and good communication techniques for the couples and families they work with. Social workers who are well liked by their clients have an advantage in that their clients are more likely to imitate their positive attitude and behavior.

Supportive Therapy

Support, in its broadest sense, consists of emotional validation, advice, guidance, feedback, material aid, and services (Ell, 1984). It is given by friends and families (informally) and by professionals (formally). How much, when, and how it is given is determined by the clients' need and their willingness to accept it as well as the capacity and willingness of other people to provide it. There have been many misperceptions in clinical social work about supportive therapy. Novices are often less attracted to it because it lacks the deep analytic interpretation of some of the more psychodynamic models and the structure of some of the behaviorally based models. It seems to them that it doesn't amount to much more than providing emotional comfort. It is, however, more than the act of comforting and reassuring emotionally overwhelmed and stressed clients. The clinician must accept the client's painful feelings unconditionally and with understanding. Supportive treatment also requires a skillful assessment of the client's current inability to cope. Secondly, the worker uncovers and reactivates preexisting strengths and works to bring them to bear on the current problems (Greenberg, 1986). The process of providing firm emotional support while exploring latent coping capacities and motivating and provoking them to action is indeed difficult and challenging clinical work. I have always imagined it as gently holding the client in one hand while poking him firmly into action with the index finger of the other hand (see Exhibit 6.4).

Acceptance

Acceptance is a social work value, but it is also a therapeutic technique. "Acceptance is not an expression of opinion about an act but an expression of goodwill toward the actor" (Woods & Hollis, 1990, p.107). People do things that are despicable. They sexually and physically abuse children (often their own). They abandon the weak in times of need. They are cruel. They may be unkempt and smelly and may elicit feelings of revulsion in the social worker. They may have no regard or respect for individual rights, property, or life.

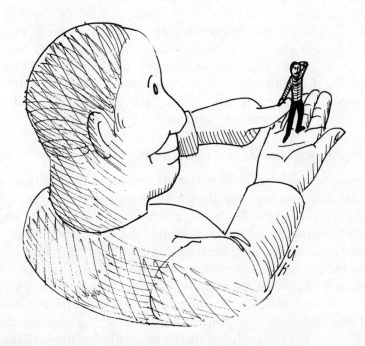

Exhibit 6.4. The social worker supports and motivates at the same time.

Being able to demonstrate an attitude of acceptance toward such clients, despite my disapproval and abhorrence of their acts, is a constant challenge. I have become appreciative of how such challenges contribute to my personal and professional growth. It is not easy to be accepting, but it is absolutely required for creating a context in which a client can change.

Emotional Release

Conventional wisdom tells us the value of "a good cry" or of "blowing off steam" to a friend. Expressing repressed emotion in a safe environment frequently relieves tension. The technical name for this process is *ventilation* or *catharsis* (a psychoanalytic concept). Although ventilation feels good, it is not usually sufficient to bring about enduring change. Nevertheless, social workers encourage ventilation as a way to build trust, reduce anxiety, and initiate exploration of the problem.

As with any therapeutic technique, it must be applied judiciously. Some clients cannot tolerate a great deal of emoting; they may become overwhelmed and decompensate (i.e., lose their ability to function or have an escalation in feelings of anxiety or depression). This is especially true for children. A release of tension is wonderfully therapeutic, but if it is unchecked it may result in increased emotional lability.

Graphic Representation of Case Information

A considerable amount of data is collected during the assessment and intervention phases of social work treatment. To be useful, the data must be organized in a way that is logical, easy to understand, and communicable to other professionals and that clearly demonstrates the relationships and issues that influence and are influenced by clients and their problems. Because problems have more than one cause (i.e., are *multi-determined*), the usual narrative descriptions are not adequate. The beauty of graphic representations of case information is that they demonstrate the multiple factors contributing to the problem and allow the clinician to share large amounts of data with clients and other professionals. Even the process of constructing graphics (e.g., the *genogram* and *ecomap*) is therapeutic. Individuals and family members report a deeper understanding of the relational or systemic aspects of their problems after constructing and discussing their genograms and ecomaps.

A genogram is similar to a family tree. Symbols are drawn (see key to Exhibit 6.5) that designate generation, sex, age, names and order of siblings, births, marriages, divorces, and deaths. Other information is determined by the referral problem. For example, if an individual has had a psychotic break, it might be useful to record the mental health and mental health treatment of family members (including hospitalizations, drugs, diagnoses, and symptoms of family members). Patterns of behavior that seem to pass from generation to generation, as well as the significance of names or order of birth, are often revealed when a genogram is constructed by an individual or family (Ingersoll-Dayton & Arndt, 1990). Clients have been known to reach out to relatives from whom they have been estranged because they are searching for missing information that their relatives may provide. Genograms can be shared in a group therapy program, handed down to younger generations of family members, or given out as gifts to selected relatives. The genogram was derived from the family systems theory of Bowen (1978) and has been adapted to social work (Hartman, 1978; Hartman & Laird, 1983; McGoldrick & Gerson, 1985). There is also a computerized version that simplifies the construction (Gerson & McGoldrick, 1985).

An ecomap is a graphic representation in which an individual or family is placed within the context of their social system. Circles represent institutions, organizations, or other factors (e.g., hobbies). Symbols represent the nature of the interrelationships between all parts of the client's social system. Like the genogram, the ecomap is a tool for getting complex data organized for assessment and intervention. It helps build rapport between client and clinician and is extremely useful for depicting a number of possible areas for goal formulation and gaining insight about the presenting problem. The genogram and the ecomap have also been used to evaluate the outcome of social work treatment. (See Exhibit 6.6 for an example of a blank ecomap, and Exhibit 6.7 for a highly detailed completed ecomap.)

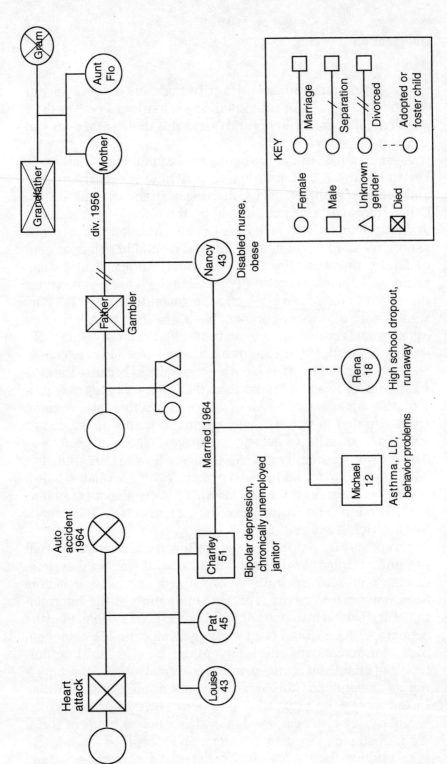

Exhibit 6.5. Genogram of the Shore family (see Dorfman, 1988b, for a full case study of this family).

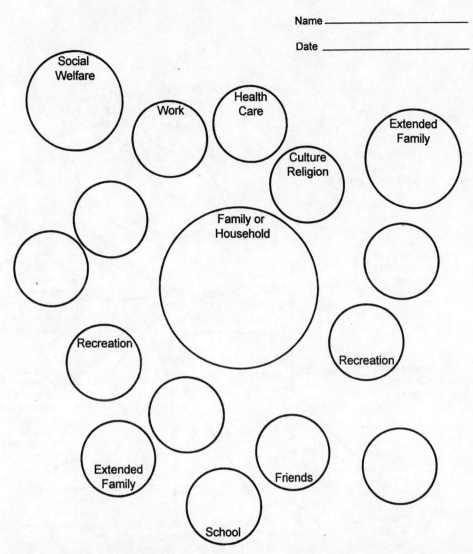

Name _____

Date _____

Fill in connections where they exist.
Indicate nature of connections with a descriptive word or by drawing different kinds of lines:
———————— for strong — — — — — for tenuous ++++++++++ for stressful.
Draw arrows along lines to signify flow of energy, resources, etc. →→→→→
Identify significant people and fill in empty circles as needed.

Exhibit 6.6. Blank ecomap. Adapted from *Family-Centered Social Work Practice* (p.160) by A. Hartman & J. Laird, 1983, New York: The Free Press. Copyright © 1983 by The Free Press. Adapted by permission.

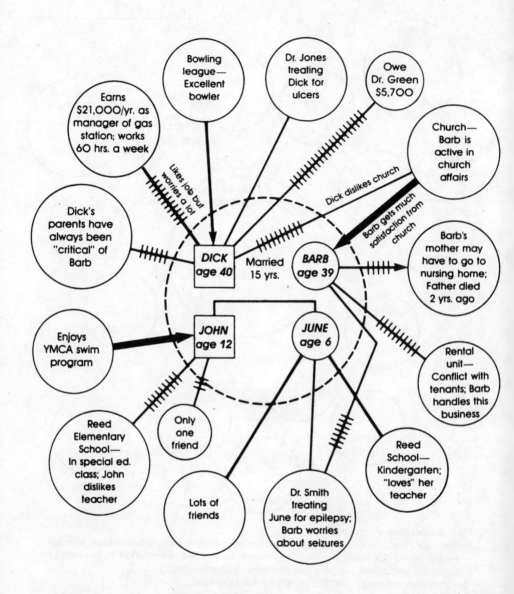

Exhibit 6.7. Example of a highly detailed ecomap. Adapted from *Techniques and Guidelines for Social Work Practice* (2nd ed., p. 223) by B.W. Sheafor, C.R. Horejsi, & G.A. Horejsi, 1991, Boston: Allyn & Bacon. Copyright 1991 by Allyn & Bacon. Adapted by permission.

Bibliotherapy

There is a huge array of self-help books on the market (e.g., Napier, 1990; Pelletier, 1992; Phelps, 1986). Many of them are written by professionals who have a gift for translating complex concepts into layperson's language and turning theories into practical suggestions for improving relationships with children or spouses or understanding one's own behavior (Burns, 1993). Other books are written by authors who have experienced and overcome or survived drug addiction, incest, depression, major illnesses, or other tragedies and who offer the wisdom gained by personal experience. These books have the potential for assisting clients and for underscoring the helping process, but they must be used advisedly. I have made it a practice to keep abreast of the "pop psychology" and self-help publications by regularly examining the recent offerings at local bookstores. Vacations are an excellent time to review these publications because of their light nature. Over the years, I have often lent these books to clients.

Children can also profit from bibliotherapy (Girard, 1991; Livingston, 1993; Mayle & Robins, 1988). When children request any of their books to be read over and over again, parents need to be helped to understand that they are not doing this to annoy but rather to "work through" conflicts or troubling feelings. For example, one little girl whose parents were separated repeatedly requested a book about a duck who went off to see the world. Her mother told me that the child showed no reaction to the apparent loss of the presence of her father. However, later, when the information about the nightly ritual of requesting the same book came out, I learned that in the center of the book was a picture of the duck with a suitcase under each wing. As the page turned to that picture, the little girl smacked the duck with her open hand. Apparently, she was "working through" or expressing feelings about her father, who also left home with suitcases under each "wing." Her request is another example of the "magic number" phenomenon.

7

TERMINATING THE THERAPEUTIC RELATIONSHIP

A TIME FOR MOURNING
OR A TIME FOR CELEBRATION?

To the untrained, most social work jargon is baffling. One exception, however, is the concept of *termination*. Most people can immediately grasp the significance of the phrase "terminating the relationship." The emotionally wrenching experience of departing appears to be universal. It is especially difficult to part from someone who is a good listener. The bond between the client and the clinician is further fixed by emotional intimacy and trust. There are at least three aspects of termination—the loss of the relationship, the recapitulation of earlier losses, and the loss of one's old self (Levinson, 1977). Termination elicits some of the most primitive and painful feelings that human beings can experience—anger, guilt, rejection, abandonment, grief, loss.[1]

---

[1]Perhaps the problem is in the language. For example, the end of high school is called graduation, not termination. It is celebrated by the ritual of "commencement" (the beginning), a time when the focus is on the accomplishment of fulfilling 12 years of educational criteria, not on grades, absences, or past infractions.

Negative emotions, however, are only part of the process. Although termination emotions are potent and common, they are "neither as universally negative nor as severe as the literature suggests" (Fortune, Pearlingi, & Rochelle, 1992, p. 172). Pride, optimism, and a sense of mastery on the part of the client and the clinician are also elicited during the process of terminating. This chapter will explore the concept and ramifications of termination.

PLANNED TERMINATION

In planned terminations, clients are told that treatment will consist of a specified number of therapeutic hours, and they are informed of the exact ending date. Later, they are assisted in working through their emotional reactions. Still later, their accomplishments and new skills are emphasized and reinforced. Finally, plans are made to ensure the maintenance of gains and continued improvement.

Clients and practitioners experience more anger, mourning, anxiety, and frustration in unplanned terminations than in planned ones. On the contrary, excitement and client determination to finish are associated with planned terminations (Cicchitto, 1983; Goldwaite, 1986; Saad, 1984). Ideally, the ending of the helping process and the fruition of treatment goals coincide. Contact in emergency-oriented settings, for instance, may be only a few hours long, ending with the stabilization of the crisis or admission to a hospital or rehabilitation setting. Clinical social work in medical settings is also brief, lasting only as long as the inpatient treatment. In an inpatient setting, termination (discharge planning) begins at admission. In child welfare and criminal justice systems, the timing of termination is likely to be directed by the court. In school settings, termination coincides with the end of the academic year.

Likewise, treatment that is covered by managed care systems is limited to a predetermined number of sessions. This has been referred to as the "financial cure"—that is, the treatment is complete when the money runs out. Managed care has given many individuals an opportunity to seek help. Unfortunately, however, clients frequently misunderstand their benefits. For example, they may believe that they are entitled to 10 sessions when, in fact, there is preauthorization for only three to five sessions. The remaining sessions will be approved only if the practitioner can document "medical necessity."

UNPLANNED TERMINATION

Clients leave treatment prematurely for a number of reasons. Among them are resistance, loss of funds (the continuation of treatment is sometimes dependent on the whim of a parent or mate who is paying for treatment but who may be unhappy with or threatened by the changes in the relative), and discouragement with progress. "No shows" are especially distressing. Reaching out to clients who terminate with no warning is the appropriate response. However, efforts to persuade the client to return are seldom effective. Time is best spent clarifying the reason for termination. Go with a hunch: "Have I offended or misunderstood you?" "Is someone or something preventing you from continuing?" "Did you expect or want a different kind of help than you are receiving?" "Are you feeling hopeless about change?" "Is transportation, child care, or money a problem?" The clinical social worker who explores these issues in a genuinely accepting and nondefensive manner is often effective in helping the client work through the obstacles to continuing treatment.

Strean (1987) suggests that clinicians may unknowingly foster premature termination. He refers to clinicians who talk too much. They are so busy "supporting," "reinforcing," and "building a relationship" that they fail to simply listen. "Many clients leave treatment prematurely without consciously knowing that they feel demeaned and weakened by the social worker's overactivity" (p. 9). Also, clinicians who suffer the same conflicts as their clients are likely to avoid discussion of their common issues. The result is little progress and early withdrawal of the client.

Premature termination is also caused by social workers who leave the agency or institution on their own initiative to take a new position. The process of separation often creates conflict for the workers who are leaving. They are acting in their own self-interest and may already be "distancing" from their old jobs. Nevertheless, they must continue to carry out their basic role of helping (Moss & Moss, 1967).

TERMINATION REACTIONS

Human beings become attached to other human beings. The prototype for that attachment is the reciprocal relationship between a mothering figure and an infant. This early, intense attachment contributes to the infant's feeling of security. The secure child rewards mother's care with contentment, which then motivates her further responsiveness to the child. Early permanent loss of that figure may result in tragic emotional and physical reactions (Bowlby, 1980). One can observe similar reactions in adults who lose mates to divorce or death. Early attachment and loss and the resolutions of those experiences may account for the wide variations in coping with present loss.

The Freudian concepts of *cathexis, decathexis,* and *recathexis* are still another way of accounting for the mourning process that follows loss. At first, person A "cathects" to the attachment figure, person B. Energy (including libido) is directed toward person B. With the loss of person B, person A must "decathect"—that is, withdraw attachment—in order to "recathect" to a new person or thing.

Freud's concept of the *narcissistic wound* might also explain the emotional reactions frequently observed during termination. Most individuals have a sense of specialness (a grandiose image) that arose in childhood. The perceived rejection or abandonment by a loved one (e.g., the social worker) can be experienced as an assault to this sense of specialness and self-esteem.

Transference fantasies that are dashed with the announcement of termination may also account for some difficulty. For example, I once treated a seriously depressed 18-year-old girl who had been adopted at birth. Her childhood had been scarred by physical, emotional, and sexual abuse. During the course of a highly volatile termination, she confessed that she sometimes believed that I was her biological mother.

Another girl, Kathy, was the offspring of a drug-addicted woman who died from an overdose when Kathy was 12 years old. Kathy had raised herself and had taken care of her mother for as long as she could remember. Kathy was withdrawn, oversolicitous, and inhibited; she rarely smiled and had no friends. At 13, her foster mother sought treatment for her at the community mental health clinic. The course of treatment was fairly successful. Kathy had, for the first time, voiced the facts of her desperate life. She began to grieve in earnest for the loss of her mother and her childhood. After six months, the social worker announced that she was leaving the agency. At first, Kathy appeared solemn and brave. After several weeks of termination work, she admitted to the clinician that even though she knew it was untrue, she liked to pretend that she was the social worker's "only" client. In other words, she was unique and special to the clinician.

Common Client Reactions to Termination

- *Acting out*. Instead of expressing anger verbally, the client "acts it out" in self-destructive behaviors, angry outbursts, defiant acts, and the like.
- *Denial*. The client shows no reaction at all or minimizes the significance of ending the relationship.
- *Return of symptoms*. Relapse occurs or brand-new problems emerge to entice the social worker to continue treatment.
- *Sadness*. Apart from such things as transference, narcissistic wounds, decathexis, and theories of attachment, the client and social worker are people who "have experienced mutual enrichment from the deep, personal, and authentic human encounter, and in a very

real sense, the self of each person has been expanded by the contacts with the other" (Hepworth & Larsen, 1993, p. 637). The ending of such a *real* relationship would result in sadness and be perceived as a loss to anyone.

- *Avoidance.* The client copes with the painful feelings of termination by leaving first, sometimes with no explanation.

- *Asks for extra sessions.* Unfortunately, for many clients, the wish to be treated outweighs the wish to be cured (Levinson, 1977). Such clients tend to become quite dependent and display minimal changes in their situations. In other cases, clients have accomplished their goals but request additional sessions in an attempt to maintain the therapeutic relationship. For instance, the client may ask to continue treatment at the social worker's new place of employment.[2]

- *Drops a "bombshell."* Sometimes, in the last moments of the last session, clients will provide rather significant information. I once had a young woman tell me, as we were about to shake hands and depart, that for the past three months she had been living in her car.

- *Initiates discussion of death or dying* (common in group work).

- *Offers dual relationship* (e.g., "We can be friends now").

- *A rekindling of feelings* that originated from previous separations and losses.

- *Feelings of betrayal* (e.g., "How can you leave when you know that I can't make it without you?"

---

[2]Clinical social workers who are leaving the agency to establish independent private practice or employment at another agency should not refer agency clients to themselves unless they have made a specific agreement with the agency they are leaving and have offered alternative options to the clients. Alternative options include (a) transferring to another social worker in the same agency, (b) continuing with the same clinician in independent private practice, (c) transferring to another agency or private practitioner, or (d) terminating treatment (NASW, 1989).

Common Clinical Social Worker Reactions to Termination

- *Guilt.* Practitioners who leave an agency often experience guilt for doing so. Common thoughts are, "No one else can help him the way I can. I really shouldn't leave." An unfortunate consequence of this guilt is that the social worker does not encourage the client to express negative feelings because such expressions would make the social worker feel worse. The practitioner may also have a sense of failing the client.
- *Avoidance.* The worker delays informing the client so that there is insufficient time to process termination reactions.
- *Offers extra sessions when unwarranted.*
- *Delays the termination.* Social workers who get their only gratification from clients tend to hold on to them too long.

Positive Reactions to Termination

The client–social worker pair often experience elation and pride. Through the therapeutic process, practitioners as well as clients obtain understanding about themselves and human behavior. Clinical social workers feel pride in their clients' successes as well as in their own skills. Other positive feelings include a sense of maturity, achievement, searching out appropriate outside therapeutic experiences and attachments, confidence in the future, and relief (Epstein, 1980; Garland, Jones, & Kolodny, 1973; Northen, 1982; Palombo, 1982). In one of the rare studies that examined termination reactions, positive feelings overshadowed negative ones. Fortune and colleagues (1992) surveyed 69 clinical social workers about termination with their most recent individual cases. The respondents reported strong positive reactions for both their clients and themselves, whereas negative reactions were weak or absent.

Factors Affecting Variations in Reactions

- *The degree of treatment success and satisfaction* (Levinson, 1977).
- *The therapeutic modality and format.* For example, brief time-limited modalities such as *task-centered treatment* (Reid, 1988) tend to limit the degree of emotional attachment and dependence developed by clients. Family and group treatment configurations tend to foster weaker termination reactions than individual formats engender. That is not to say, however, that no attachment occurs.
- *Previous experience with loss.* Although in some cases early loss may help clients cope with current loss, in other situations the emotions from earlier loss are unresolved and may be reexperienced in the present.
- *Current life situation.* A crisis in employment, school, marriage, or family may leave the client with less coping capacity to handle the stress of termination.
- *The meaning of the therapeutic relationship to the client.* Yalom (1980) wrote that the tragedy of psychotherapy is that the therapist is always more important to the client than the client is to the therapist. Although this is arguable, it does highlight the fact that one must be cognizant of how clients perceive the relationship and the importance of that relationship to the client.
- *Cultural tradition.* For example, many Asian cultures maintain formal, deferential relationships with professional people. Although the social worker's departure may sadden such clients, they are not likely to express it in any overt way—and in fact may be well defended against any strong emotion.
- *Characteristic coping mechanisms.* I recall, for example, a high school girl I was counseling. Her rebellious behavior caused constant havoc at school and at home. Because she wanted to maintain her tough exterior, she

never allowed herself to cry. Whenever tears began to well up, she would say "Be a rock" over and over to herself until she regained a stoic composure. On the occasion of our last meeting, she was indeed "a rock."

- *Personality traits or features.* Clients are true to their personalities. An individual who has perfected the art of manipulation may use that skill to get treatment extended. Narcissistic personalities, on the other hand, tend to react to termination announcements with little distress and a request to know "Who is going to be my next worker?"

Termination Goals

- All or most of the agreed-upon treatment goals have been achieved.
- Negative reactions have been worked through. Helping clients express their feelings is a priority. Often, reluctant clients need only a small prompt to help them give voice to their feelings. For instance, a clinician might say, "Saying good-bye brings up a lot of different feelings for most people. I have found that the best way to deal with such feelings is to talk about them." This normalizes the client's feelings, positive and negative, and suggests the usefulness of discussion. It is only where negative responses dominate that intensive grief and mourning should be emphasized" (Fortune et al., 1992).
- The therapeutic effort is perceived as worth the time and energy spent. Acknowledge and reinforce positive emotions. Encourage expressions of acceptance regarding the client–social worker relationship and the completed goals as well as the disappointments.
- The client has an increased capacity for problem solving.
- The client has an increased understanding of his or her own motivations—and human behavior in general. The

client has obtained the language for discussing and observing the self.

- The client has a sense of self-efficacy. Reviewing the accomplishments and how the client attained them reinforces confidence and solidifies the gains (Levinson, 1977). One technique that captures the joy of accomplishment is what I call "the best of..." I invite the client to join me in recalling the highlights of our work together, including achievements, learnings, and faux pas.
- The client feels valued and respected.
- The development of a plan to maintain gains and to continue to work on problems.
- Evaluation (see Chapter 8).

The Significance of Ritual

In the beginning, it looked hopeless. Sharon was drug addicted, with no means of physical, emotional, or financial support. Her 2-year-old twins were in foster care. She appeared to be unmotivated. There was little hope of family reunification. One year later, Sharon was drug-free and attending secretarial school. She had completed a parent-training course and attended Narcotics Anonymous religiously. The court allowed her to have frequent contact with the children.

The helping process had been fraught with setbacks and frustrations. Regaining custody of the twins was now a possibility, but there was more work to be done. The one constant in Sharon's life was June, her social worker from the Child Welfare Department. However, June had accepted a new job and would be relocating to another city. Their termination reflected the course of treatment. It was difficult and marked with numerous crises. Nevertheless, all the bases were covered—that is, feelings were expressed, the work was reviewed, and new skills acknowledged and reinforced. Plans were made to maintain Sharon's accomplishments and to continue to fulfill the court's requirements. The only thing left for Sharon and June to do was to note and celebrate their work and their relationship. Sharon suggested a diploma. With the help of computer software, June created a diploma that acknowledged that Sharon Jones now had her "head screwed on straight."

I always let the client know that we will mark the occasion. Merely saying "We will have to make our last session special in some way" plants a seed. Once hearing this, clients often make suggestions that are personally significant. If such an idea doesn't emerge, I might suggest one. Children always like "parties" with cake and ice cream or cookies and punch. Children and adults have asked permission to bring in a camera to take photographs.

Termination may be particularly difficult for a child. Children do not tend to initiate endings. When it happens to them, it has the potential to increase feelings of helplessness. Termination may also be painful for those children who have had multiple losses. Children's therapeutic relationships tend to be less marked by transference, and thus the loss of the worker is perceived as a "real" loss (Elbow, 1987).

An effective technique that facilitates the termination process for a child and involves the child and the social worker is the *memory book* (Elbow, 1987). The creation of a memory book allows the child and worker to review the purpose of the treatment and encourages them to discuss the meaning of the relationship, the child's accomplishments, and the impending loss. A unique and useful feature of this process is that the child learns what he or she has contributed to the social worker.

The social worker prepares an outline of the book, defining the major issues that were dealt with during the helping process. Elbow (1987) suggests that each page should have no more than two topics and have sufficient space for the child's response or illustration.

Creating a Memory Book

- The first topic (or question) should address the reason that they came together. The worker encourages the child to list or draw pictures showing the problems that brought them together.

- The worker asks the child to recall happy, sad, or angry times.
- Next they write together or separately about how those feelings were handled.
- They recall specific problems and struggles and the way they came to be resolved. It is important to record what both gained and learned from these struggles.
- The book concludes with a statement about what the worker gained from the relationship and will remember most about the child. Finally, the child writes a statement or draws about what he or she gained from the relationship and will remember most about the worker (Elbow, 1987).

Farewell Gifts

A small gift such as a plant or book may be especially meaningful. The plant, a symbol of growth, helps to end the work optimistically. Books should be chosen for the messages they impart. For example, the message of Sheldon Kopp's (1976) book, *If You Meet a Buddha on the Road, Kill Him!* is that although gurus (e.g., teachers and social workers) enlighten us, a time comes when one is ready to handle life's challenges by oneself. At that point, the Buddha is not only superfluous but is an obstacle to continued personal growth.

TRANSFERRING CLIENTS

When a social worker leaves an agency, some of his or her clients may have to be transferred to another practitioner. Let's use Sharon as a good example again, only this time she is not ready to terminate. She needs the continued support of social work treatment. Like all therapeutic maneuvers, transfer requires planning. "Ideally toward the end of therapy with the original worker, the new therapist can be introduced and join one session or part of a session (not the last one, of course, which should be reserved for worker and client to say their final good-byes). Sometimes, because of the pressure of time or the worker's own ambivalence about leaving, transfers are too quickly or casually managed" (Woods & Hollis, 1990, p. 450).

The badly handled termination and improperly managed transfer is not without consequences. Anger and grief that are not dealt with in the closing sessions with the old worker rear their heads again, in some fashion, with the new worker. Sharon, in this instance, did not have a satisfactory termination before her transfer to another social worker. Later, she developed a cluster of symptoms labeled "the transfer syndrome" (Keith, 1966, cited in Wapner, Klein, Friedlander, & Andrasik, 1986). Common manifestations of the syndrome among adults are depressive equivalents (e.g., somatic symptoms, a loss of interest in the content of sessions, pleas for changes in medications or appointment times). Some clients ventilate anger by criticizing the previous therapist but defend against the painful grief that accompanies their loss. Thus, before work can begin with the new clinician, there is often some "mopping up" to do.

8

CLINICAL PRACTICE EVALUATION

by Kimberly Cash, M.S.W.

By the time clinical social work students graduate from an accredited social work program, they have some mastery of the skills required to conduct psychosocial assessments and therapeutic interventions. They are aware (often painfully) of the crucial issues that characterize the termination phase and are prepared to manage them. There is, however, one element of competent clinical social work practice that has yet to be addressed—clinical evaluation. This phase of practice informs the clinical social worker about whether or not the client's situation has improved.

Without a systematic method for evaluation, the practitioner's clinical judgment and intuition—or the client's self-report alone—must be relied on to determine improvement. When the school-phobic child returns to the classroom, the batterer stops hitting his wife, and the chronically unemployed individual retains a job, change seems obvious. However, other problems (e.g., depression, low self-esteem, or obsessive rumination) are less easily discerned.

Implicit or subjective methods of evaluating a client's progress, though certainly part of the natural rhythm of clinical practice, are often fraught with pitfalls. One drawback is that if clinicians have given little attention to specifying or documenting the client's problem, treatment, or response to treatment, they are limited in their ability to discuss the client's progress with precision and accuracy. Even the most seasoned clinician may fall prey to certain "errors in personal human inquiry" (Rubin & Babbie, 1993, p. 11) that lead to inaccurate, premature, or ineffective treatment decisions .[1]

In addition, the client, the client's family, the clinician's employer or supervisor, or outside funding sources desire "accountability"—that is, concrete evidence that the client is improving. Demonstrating accountability requires more concrete information than what is gained by informal evaluation of one's practice (Briar, 1973; Nuehring & Pascone, 1986).

This chapter will address the most frequently utilized practice-evaluation method, single-subject design. The emphasis will be on the emergence of single-subject design and its adoption by the social work profession, its utility as a tool for day-to-day clinical practice, and descriptions of procedures.

HISTORICAL REVIEW OF
APPROACHES TO PRACTICE EVALUATION

For over a century, research in the social sciences has focused on increasing our knowledge of human behavior and examining the impact of therapeutic interventions (Bloom, 1983). The *case study method* led to the first groundbreaking developments in this quest for understanding. Examples of pioneering case studies familiar to most students include the work of Jean Piaget (1952) and Sigmund Freud (1963). Their discoveries laid the foundation for learning theory, cognitive theory, and psychoanalytic theory (Lefrancois, 1993), all of which inform eclectic clinical social work practice.

Despite the value of case studies for promoting discussion

---

[1]These include *inaccurate observation, overgeneralization, selective observation, made-up information, illogical reasoning, premature closure of inquiry,* and *ego involvement in understanding* (Rubin & Babbie, 1993).

and reflection among colleagues, the wide variation and subjective nature of such studies became unattractive to an increasingly sophisticated scientific community (Barlow & Hersen, 1984). In the second half of the 20th century, the development of statistical theory and the increasing precision of scientific research contributed to the decline in the use of the case study method.

Other early attempts to systematically evaluate clinical practice relied upon *classical group designs* (Bloom, 1983). This approach reoriented the focus from the individual to the group and typically involved gathering information on two groups of clients, all of whom were dealing with a particular problem or had been diagnosed with a common disorder. Clients were randomly assigned to one of the two groups; those in the *control group* would go untreated while those in the *experimental group* would be exposed to some type of intervention. After data for the two groups had been compared, any differences identified in the groups' outcomes would be attributed to the treatment method.

Classical group designs were also subjected to intense scrutiny as a result of a series of events in the 1960s and 1970s. For example, a series of studies impugning the effectiveness of casework created a fury among researchers (Fischer, 1973; Wood, 1978). Reactions to subsequent examinations of casework included the claim that the flaw was not in casework but rather in the methods for evaluating casework. Group designs were criticized as being not narrow enough in focus to assess individual progress in treatment (Reid & Hanrahan, 1982). Studies also revealed that only a minority of social workers even employed the group-design method. Most clinicians simply assumed that their interventions were producing positive results (Blythe & Briar, 1985; Kirk, Osmalov, & Fischer, 1976).

The dilemma confronting researchers and practitioners alike was captured by Florence Haselkorn (1978):

We are left in the position that although in principle we should verify our claim, and in principle outcome evaluation is necessary if we are to operate without the self-deception of impassioned believers, we are as yet unable to establish with scientific rigor that our efforts are effective *or* ineffective. (p. 335)

This dilemma led to a reconsideration of the appropriateness of group designs for practice evaluation. A call rang out for a method that could meet the variety of demands that had accumulated during the history of scientific inquiry with regard to effective practice evaluation (Briar, 1973). By the late 1970s, single-subject design (which was drawn from the field of experimental psychology and from the techniques pioneered by behaviorist B. F. Skinner) was being heralded as the solution to the "crisis of accountability" faced by clinical practitioners (Kazdin, 1982; Newman & Turem, 1974).

SINGLE-SUBJECT DESIGN

Single-subject design has been widely promoted as a "user-friendly" technology that effectively integrates research and day-to-day clinical practice (Barlow & Hersen, 1984; Bloom, 1983; Bloom, Fischer, & Orme, 1995; Jayaratne & Levy, 1979; Kazdin, 1982; Tripodi, 1994). Although we have chosen to use the term "single-subject" for the sake of simplicity, this method has been variously labeled "single-case," "single-system," and "clinical research" design. Regardless of the terminology employed or the subtleties of the discourse surrounding this evaluative method, its distinguishing feature is that the focus of study is a single client "unit" (an individual, couple, family, or group).

In single-subject design, the comparison is between a single client's measurements before treatment and measurements at various points during treatment, whereas in group designs the comparison is between a group of clients who receive treatment and a group of clients who do not.

One of the first steps in conducting the most basic of single-subject studies, *the basic A-B design*, is to establish the client's *baseline*. This is a measurement of the client's presenting problem (or *target problem*) before any intervention or treatment has been implemented. Also critical is the identification of the client's treatment goal (or *outcome goal*). Following introduction of the intervention, the clinician continues to collect information about the client's target problem until treatment is terminated. Data gathered during the baseline and intervention phases of treatment are then compared, allowing the clinician to assess the client's progress on an ongoing basis and, when necessary, make adjustments in the treatment plan.

Uses of Single-Subject Design

There are more than a dozen variations of the single-subject research design, each providing the practitioner with different information (Tripodi, 1994). Some versions are more complex and more scientifically rigorous than others, requiring more expertise and more time to conduct. The choice of a particular design will therefore depend upon the clinicians' priorities and goals as they set out to evaluate their practices. For clinicians who desire immediate and practical feedback that helps them track their clients' progress, clarify treatment procedures, and respond to demands for accountability, an *evaluative* (Thyer, 1993) or *preexperimental* (Kazdin, 1982) single-subject design is ideal.[2]

The A-B design is the foundation of all single-subject designs. The "A" refers to the baseline phase of the study and the "B" denotes the intervention phase. The question this version of the single-subject study seeks to answer is: "Did the client (or *client unit*) improve over the course of treatment?

Given the introductory nature of this discussion, we will not take up the debate over the uses of single-subject design or the methodologies employed in more complex designs. The proce-

---

[2]If the goal in conducting a single-subject study is to determine whether the intervention was effective, or if an intervention that helped one client will be successful with subsequent clients, clinicians will need to employ an *experimental* (Thyer, 1993) version of a single-subject design. The experimental design is needed to determine if the change was *caused* by the treatment.

dures for conducting a single-subject study, outlined in the next
section, will be limited to the basic A-B design. For those
interested in more thorough descriptions and discussions of
this method, we recommend the most recent works by Bloom
and colleagues (1995), Barlow and Hersen (1984), and Blythe,
Tripodi, and Briar (1994).

PROCEDURES FOR CONDUCTING A SINGLE-SUBJECT STUDY [3]

Perhaps the greatest appeal of single-subject design is that it
mirrors the phases of direct clinical practice. Numerous texts
and articles addressing single-subject design over the past two
and a half decades share a common approach to conducting
such studies (Barlow & Hersen, 1984; Blythe & Tripodi, 1989;
Bloom and colleagues, 1995; Jayaratne & Levy, 1979; Kazdin,
1982; Tripodi, 1994).

Selecting a Target Behavior

Implementing a single-subject study begins in the assessment
phase of treatment. As discussed in Chapter 5, one of the key
tasks in conducting a biopsychosocial assessment is to identify
the client's presenting problem. A thorough understanding of
the presenting problem may require several meetings. This is
especially true when clients are unsure about the nature of their
difficulties or when they are struggling with a number of
different problems at the same time.

The first step in conducting a single-subject study is to
operationally define the client's presenting problem in *concrete*, *precise*, and *observable* terms. This translates the
presenting problem into a target problem. Some target problems are clear-cut and easy to define. For example, "insomnia"

---

[3]The literature displays wide variation in the terminology and styles of
description regarding single-subject design procedures. The terms used
here were chosen in the interests of clarity and to reflect a consensus among
the authors about components required to conduct a basic A-B study.

might be operationalized as "2 to 3 hours of sleep per night." Other clients present complaints that are related to an internal state and are more difficult to describe or define. For example, "anxiety" afflicts many people, but manifests itself differently. For some people, an increased level of anxiety may be associated with overt behaviors, such as "binge eating" or "overexercising." Other clients identify troubling physiological symptoms such as "racing heartbeat" or "sweaty palms." In cases in which the problem is more subjectively experienced, the clinician assists the client in identifying specific *indicators* of his or her anxiety that can easily be monitored over the course of treatment.

Selecting the Outcome Measure

Another task within the assessment phase of practice is the identification of an initial treatment goal. The primary goal of all clinical practice is to help clients find relief from their problems. For the purpose of practice evaluation, however, this more general goal must be translated into an *outcome goal*, which is typically a desire for an *increase* or a *reduction* in the frequency (how many), magnitude (how much), or duration (how long) of the client's target behavior.

Let us say, for example, that the clinical social worker has identified an adolescent client's target problem as "poor grades," the most significant indicator of which is the client's failure, four out of every five school days, to turn in his homework. The outcome goal in working with this client would therefore be to help him improve his grades, measured as an increase in the frequency with which he completes and turns in his assignments.

Methods of Measurement

The three most common methods for conducting a basic single-subject design include *direct observation, standardized measures*, and *client self-report* (Blythe & Tripodi, 1989; Fischer & Corcoran, 1994; Hersen & Bellack, 1981).

Direct Observation

When a client enters treatment hoping to change some aspect of behavior, direct observation of the behavior is a simple and accessible approach to measurement. Because the observer could be the practitioner, a significant person in the client's life (such as a parent, teacher, or spouse), or perhaps even the client, it is crucial that the behavior being targeted has been specified clearly enough so that everyone involved will be able to identify the same indicators.

Standardized Measures

The practitioner may select a *standardized instrument* for measurement in circumstances in which it will be useful to compare the client to a wider group of people who have experienced the same problem, or when it is important to have a *straightforward* and *rapid* method of monitoring the client's progress. Examples of these instruments include question-naires, tests, inventories, and checklists. Because standardized measures are administered and scored in the same fashion by all practitioners, this method has the added appeal of having met standards of methodological adequacy (i.e., they are both reliable and valid).

Client Self-Report

In cases where the client's goal for treatment relates to an *internal* state, the most appropriate strategy for measurement is *client self-report*. Thoughts, feelings, and beliefs—for example, "hopelessness" or "guilt"—cannot always be operationalized in behavioral terms.

One particularly useful method of self-report is a *self-anchored rating scale*. The social worker and the client work together on developing this scale to meet the specific needs of the client's situation. It can be used to measure the intensity of a problem. Over time, it can assist the client in understanding the connection between internal feelings and external behaviors.

Establishing a Baseline

Once the target problem has been selected, the outcome goal of treatment has been identified, and the clinician has decided upon a strategy for measurement, all of the tools necessary for implementing the single-subject study are in place.

The next task is to establish the *baseline* of the study to identify a *stable pattern* in the occurrence of this problem to provide a means of comparison once the client has been exposed to an intervention. The number of measures taken and the amount of time needed for establishing a baseline will vary according to the needs of the client, the policies and procedures of the practice setting, and the complexity of the measurement strategy.

There may be situations in which delaying an intervention to establish a baseline measure would interfere with ethical or administrative priorities in working with a client. When evaluation goals conflict with practice realities, particularly when a client is at risk for further deterioration or suffering, the practitioner may need to adjust the evaluation approach. If, for instance, a client disclosed in an initial assessment interview that she had been contemplating suicide and a clinician decided to wait until the following appointment to establish a baseline for the frequency of the client's suicidal ideation, the client would obviously be put at great risk, and the clinician would be violating her ethical responsibilities. This rather extreme example was chosen for the sake of illustrating a point. In this situation, the clinician would want to consider an alternative method of determining the extent of the client's despair. The practitioner may reconstruct the past by developing a *retrospective baseline*. Information used to develop a retrospective baseline can be obtained from a number of sources (with the client's permission), including client records, interviews or questionnaires conducted with friends, family, or colleagues of the client, or from the client's memory.

Intervention Phase

Once the social worker has developed and introduced the intervention, he or she will then systematically and consistently record the extent and severity of the client's target problem. For the duration of the client's involvement in treatment, the practitioner may reflect upon the data gathered and, in consultation with the client, adjust the intervention strategy if the client does not appear to be making progress toward the goal.

Assessing Treatment Outcome

The final step in conducting clinical practice evaluation is to compare and analyze the data that have been so carefully gathered. Interpreting the data gathered in a single-subject study typically involves a form of visual analysis such as a *graph*. The graph helps to identify patterns or changes in the client's target problems and shows whether the client has successfully met his or her outcome goal. Having successfully implemented the single-subject study, the clinician is now able to answer the question posed at the opening of this discussion: "Did the client improve during the course of treatment?" If you recall the earlier discussion of the various uses of single-subject designs, the basic A-B design will not tell the practitioner if the treatment he or she selected *caused* the client to improve. That is an experimental question. The results of the basic A-B study are based on *clinical significance*, defined as "the perception of an important result of treatment" (Jayaratne, 1990, p. 273). If the data collected over the course of treatment reveal that a change in the client's target problem has occurred, and the client, practitioner, or other significant persons in the client's life perceive this as a meaningful change, then it is possible to consider the client's treatment a success.

Over the past two and a half decades, a number of researchers and educators have joined in exhorting clinicians to implement more rigorous single-subject studies in order to broaden the knowledge base of the social work profession and to respond to increasing demands for accountability (Blythe & Briar, 1985; Briar, 1977). We would like to join those ranks and encourage novice clinical social workers—particularly those who grimace at the mere mention of "research"—to see single-subject design as a responsibility and an opportunity (not a constraint) for conscientious and fruitful practice.

9

THINGS THEY DON'T TEACH YOU IN PROFESSIONAL SCHOOL

PERPLEXING AND SENSITIVE QUESTIONS

A discipline's theoretical framework and practice methods are communicated to neophytes through the words emanating from behind podiums and from assigned readings. Most disciplines (e.g., law, medicine, nursing, social work), however, have also developed field components or "internships" so that the "green peas" can obtain the experience and wisdom that cannot be obtained by book learning alone.[1]

The following questions regarding the practice of clinical social work have been asked by social work interns in the field and within the confines of a supervisor/supervisee relationship. Few of these issues are addressed in traditional textbooks or lectures.

---

[1]*Green peas* is the affectionate term used by Jane Kurohara, MSW, to refer to her first-year social work students. Kurohara has been a field instructor at the Department of Social Welfare, University of California, Los Angeles, for 24 years and has been a social worker for 41 years.

What Do I Do About a Sexually Seductive Client?

Clients are motivated to seduce their therapists for all sorts of reasons. Among them are these:

- To gratify sexual desire (Edelwich & Brodsky, 1991)
- To divert attention from treatment issues
- To manipulate
- To gain power or equalize the perceived power differential in the relationship (Edelwich & Brodsky, 1991)
- To satisfy fantasies related to the idealization of the therapist and "infantile sexual desires" (Applebaum & Jorgenson, 1991, p. 1469).

Among the choices for the clinician vis-à-vis a seductive client are flight,[2] acquiescence, and "a dispassionate attempt to understand the meaning of the behavior and an attempt to use it in the client's behalf" (Gareffa & Neff, 1974, p. 116). The NASW Code of Ethics is unambiguous: "The social worker should under no circumstances engage in sexual activities with clients" (NASW, 1993b, Article II:5; see Appendix B and Exhibit 9.1).

It is difficult to offer remedies for client seductiveness. Each case is different. Depending on the situation, the intervention may range from setting limits for the client to a straightforward discussion of the client's seductiveness. The purpose of the latter would be to help the client observe his or her own behavior, gaining insight about its ramifications. An exploration of how seductive behavior may or may not have served the client in the past and present might also be discussed. Most important is for the clinician to be aware of his or her contribution to the sexual dynamics of the situation and to be absolutely

---

[2]The prototype for therapist flight from the seductive client is Joseph Breuer. Breuer, a colleague of Freud, was treating a hysterical female patient, Anna O. Much to his dismay, Anna O. proclaimed her love and asked him to have a baby with her. So distraught was he with this situation that Breuer terminated treatment and went off on a second honeymoon with his wife, who soon after became pregnant (Strean, 1993).

Exhibit 9.1. The seductive client.

certain that he or she is not giving double messages to the client. If the client asks for sex, the response must be nonrejecting but firm.

What Do I Do if I Become Sexually Attracted or Aroused by a Client?

Most clinicians, at some point(s) in their careers, will become sexually attracted to a client. This statement is based on a survey of practicing therapists (Pope, Keith-Speigel, & Tabachnick, 1986) as well as my own experience as a practitioner and clinical supervisor. In addition to being aware of clients' seductive behavior, practitioners must be aware of any erotic attraction to a client and understand the implications and dynamics of sexuality in the treatment relationship.

Strean (1993) points out that therapists who inhibit, deny, and repress erotic feelings toward clients and therapists who act out their wishes by engaging in sexual relations are not all that different from each other. In both situations, they are attempting to cope with anxiety while suffering a great deal. In addition, "neither the repressed practitioner nor the sexually acting-out practitioner is substantially helping his or her patients!" (p. xi). Strean suggests that the wish to have sex is universal. If one accepts such feelings as natural, (see Bullis, 1995, pp. 73–79, for clinical disorders that predispose practitioners to sexual misconduct with their clients) less anxiety is generated, thus reducing the possibility of either repression or acting out.

An issue I have never seen addressed in a textbook or in the classroom is the social worker's awareness (often with much guilt and discomfort) that he or she is becoming sexually aroused (during a session) in response to discussion of sexual material. Counter to what some may believe, professional training does not turn off human physiology. It is best to simply note the arousal as an interesting but irrelevant reaction and continue the therapeutic process.

We Are Warned Against Having Dual Relations With Clients. What Are They? Is It Ever Okay?

The social worker's relationship with the client must be unconflicted. Roles are clear. The client receives ethical, confidential, and competent treatment, and the worker is paid for the service he or she delivers. "Dual relations refers to conflicted loyalties caused by conflicting roles between social worker and client" (Bullis, 1995, p. xii).

Dual relations occur when workers engage in the following activities with their clients:

- Sexual contact
- Bartering and other business arrangements. Bartering consists of trading services or goods (instead of cash payment) for social work treatment. When it occurs, it is usually in private practice settings. Bartering allows clients with insufficient funds to obtain access to ser-

vices. It may provide the clinician with a service he or she could not otherwise afford (e.g., landscaping, piano lessons for a child). Although there are advantages, there are also disadvantages. Bartering changes the quality of the client–worker relationship. In the course of the exchange, the bartering client may enter the social worker's home, become acquainted with family members, and be privy to the more intimate details of the social worker's life.[3] The same can be said of most other business agreements. The nature of business is such that one's own self-interest almost always supersedes the interest of the other party. Entering into joint business ventures with clients creates conflicts of interest and puts the helping process in jeopardy.

• Accepting close friends or family members as clients.[4] Although rapport is already established and time saved because such clients and their situations are already known to the social worker, the situation is fraught with risk. There is the possibility of loyalty and friendship overriding what Bullis (1995) calls "regulatory schemes" (p. 119). In other words, there is the tendency to grant special favors that are counter to agency policy. There is also the danger of a less positive outcome because of diminished professional credibility. Friends and family

---

[3]Many clinicians have managed this with no obvious problems. Milton Erickson, for example, saw people in his home, where they had the opportunity to become acquainted with his children. However, it does increase risk for problems—for example, some clients may expect to have a social relationship after termination or may have a more difficult time with termination because of the level of intimacy created by entering the clinician's personal domain. (See Rappoport, 1982, for a discussion of bartering in psychotherapy.)

[4]Bullis (1995) proposes two "tests" to determine whether friends and family members are too close to counsel. "If friends and family members are uncomfortable about paying for services or if the social worker is uncomfortable about asking for payment, the individuals are too 'close' to receive treatment" (p. 120). Second, if the social worker fears "disclosing the dual relations to a supervisor, licensing board, peer supervisor, or other colleague," (p.120) the individuals are too "close" to receive treatment.

members have seen the social worker at his or her most vulnerable and are well aware of his or her short-comings.

- Socializing. Social workers have attended clients' weddings and graduations. However, most clinicians agree that socializing (e.g., inviting clients to a personal party, going out to eat with them after a session, or accepting an invitation to a special event) is rarely ethical (Borys, 1988; cited in Herlihy & Corey, 1992). The new social roles created by these activities may undermine the helping process—for example, by introducing social obligations and responsibility into the therapeutic relationship.

Dual relationships complicate an already difficult task. They put the relationship, the well-being of the client, and the professional reputation of the social worker at risk. It is a situation in which the risks far outweigh any possible benefits.

Is Clinical Social Work Dangerous?

Social workers offer help, but they also represent authority, and as such are often targets of rage (Schultz, 1989). Thus, many social workers experience physical, verbal, and property abuse at the hands of the people they are trying to help. Physical violence toward social workers, for example, has been reported in mental health and health settings, correctional settings, child protective services, substance abuse programs, and handi-capped services (Schultz, 1989).

Potential for client violence toward social workers is associated with the following:

- The influence of substance abuse and addiction
- Mental illness
- Cuts in the fiscal base of social services (Schultz, 1989)
- Vulnerability (a passive, timid, or fearful worker)
- Client feelings of loss of power or control (Kaplan & Wheeler, 1983)

- Client history of violence (see Kaplan & Wheeler, 1983, for a discussion of predictors of violence)

To decrease the potential for violence, social work students and seasoned practitioners are trained to recognize and defuse behaviors that foreshadow aggression. However, research has demonstrated that the amount of violence prevention and management training in schools of social work and in health and social service settings remains seriously deficient (Tully, Kroff, & Price, 1991).

What Do I Do to Keep Safe?

The following guidelines (adapted from Sheafor and colleagues, 1994, pp. 253–255) should be observed when working with potentially violent clients:

- Never enter a situation known to be dangerous without consulting with others. Encountering individuals who possess firearms or other weapons or individuals with a history of violent behavior is unsafe. Meeting unfamiliar clients in nonpublic or isolated places is also dangerous. In these situations, the social worker should call for police protection.
- The client records of potentially violent individuals should be color coded or flagged in some way so that a social worker new to the case would be forewarned of the danger. It also makes sense for agencies to develop an emergency communication code (e.g., a seemingly innocuous phrase) that all staff understand is a veiled request for assistance.
- Home visits require particular care. Keep the office informed about your whereabouts and check in by phone according to a prearranged schedule. Before entering a home, do a safety check (e.g., note the escape routes).
- A perceived intrusion may trigger violent behavior in persons who are prone to such outbursts. Never move

through a doorway in response to "Come in" unless you can see the person who is speaking and the person can see you. It is vital to avoid being mistaken for someone else.

- Guns are usually kept in the bedroom, and other potentially dangerous weapons are often in the kitchen. If you are in the home of a dangerous person who is threatening you and moving toward one of these rooms, leave immediately.

- When an aggressive client becomes afraid or angry, do whatever you can do to defuse the anger. This includes remaining composed and speaking in a gentle, soothing manner. Do not argue, lecture, or advise. Allow the person to "ventilate" to drain off the intensity of feelings.

- Watch for signs of imminent attack, such as flaring nostrils, dilated pupils, pulsing veins, teeth grinding, fist clenching, and crouching of the upper body. Do not turn your back on an angry client.

- Do not attempt to disarm a client with a weapon. Calmly explain that you intend no harm, and slowly back away. Call the police.

- Social workers who work in dangerous areas are best advised to seek guidance from others who are experienced in self-protection. Most important is to not overestimate your ability to handle the situation or underestimate the dangerousness of the potentially violent client.

I Sometimes Feel Like a Police Officer Instead of a Social Worker. Is This a Proper Role for a Clinical Social Worker?

Social workers take tremendous pride in what they do. It is not a high-status profession, nor is it glamorous or lucrative. Many who are drawn to it have been natural helpers since childhood. Others have overcome individual and family difficulties or health and mental health problems and wish to "give back" in appreciation of the help they received. Still others have been inspired by helpers they have encountered. Social workers characterize themselves as kind and caring, their work as benevolent, their professional values as humanitarian. They seek to be ever more accepting, understanding, empathic, sensitive, and insightful.

It is therefore not surprising that when social workers are confronted with the "social control"[5] aspects of their jobs, they feel that it is incompatible with their aims. Terms such as *authority, power, control, coercion,* and *force* may be held in contempt. The problem is that not all clinical social workers have been well schooled in this particular social work role. They may not have a grounding in the three R's of social control—rationality, reason, and responsibility.[6]

There are clients who do not respond to counseling, guidance, support, concrete services, or any other social work intervention. Such clients must be made to understand that their actions or lack of action will result in, for example, loss of child custody or incarceration. Even in the case of a client who has the potential to respond, it may be impractical or dangerous to wait for a "cure." For example, a father may have good intentions and demonstrate genuine remorse about sexually abusing his daughter, but his behavior suggests that he is still incapable of inhibiting his impulses. Few would argue that the father must be removed from the home, forcibly if necessary, to protect the child from further victimization. The workers who carry out these decisions (e.g., in child welfare or correctional settings) are acting as agents of social control. They are enforcing the limits of behavior outlined by law to maintain order, social norms, and values. In essence, they are *helping* through

---

[5]"Whenever a social worker...engages in an activity to modify or set boundaries on human contact according to valued norms, that person is engaging in social control" (Cowger & Atherton, 1974, p. 457).

[6]Rationality suggests a well-thought-out action uninfluenced by emotion. Reason suggests that there is a justification for the action. Responsibility suggests that someone will be accountable for seeing that the norms, values, rules, or laws of society are carried out.

controlling (which should, of course, still be done with respect and caring).

When Is a Clinical Social Worker Required to Report Information About Clients to Authorities or Others?

Sometimes clients tell social workers about their intent to harm or kill others. The appropriate response to these threats is not always clear. Every clinical social worker needs to study the legal rulings that pertain to their state and seek consultation when faced with client threats to other people. There are two basic dilemmas regarding reporting:

- Acting in accordance with the ethical and legal responsibilities to clients (e.g., confidentiality) versus fulfilling legal obligations to society
- Balancing the welfare of the individual client (e.g., preserving the therapeutic relationship) against the concerns for the welfare of society (e.g., protecting innocent children)

The Tarasoff Decision

In 1969, Prosenjit Poddar was an outpatient at the student health services at the University of California, Berkeley. Poddar informed his counselor, psychologist Lawrence Moore, that he was going to kill Tatiana Tarasoff when she returned from a trip to Brazil.

Believing that Poddar was a threat and required commitment to a mental hospital for observation, Moore consulted with other university counselors and then informed the campus police, who took Poddar into custody for questioning. He convinced the police that he was "rational" and promised to stay away from Tarasoff, so they released him. Moore followed up his initial call to the campus police with a formal letter requesting assistance. Moore's supervisor later requested that the letter be returned and that Moore destroy his case notes.

Neither Tarasoff's parents nor anyone close to her was informed of the threat to her life. Shortly after her return to the United States, Prosenjit Poddar killed Tatiana Tarasoff at her home in Berkeley.

Her parents filed a suit against the Board of Regents and the employees of the university for their failure to warn them or their daughter. After a dismissal by a lower court, the California Supreme Court ruled in favor of the parents in 1976 (*Tarasoff v. Regents of the University of California,* 1976). The ruling required that therapists breach confidentiality in cases where the welfare of others is in danger. It was decided that therapists have a "duty to warn" intended victims. In a second ruling, this was changed to a "duty to protect."

Probably the most common error in such instances is that social workers believe that they are *required* to *warn* third parties of the danger, whereas the wording is *duty to protect.* As a way of protecting third parties, one legal scholar has recommended seeking involuntary commitment for violent patients who refuse to enter the hospital, even when these patients do not meet the usual criteria for commitment (Kopels & Kagle, 1993). The *Tarasoff* ruling is still debated and is often the center of controversy. A number of state courts have not yet ruled on applications of *Tarasoff,* which means that practitioners remain in a state of uncertainty about the nature of their duty to protect or warn (Fulero, 1988). One of the best of the recent articles that responds to *Tarasoff's* ethical, legal, and practical ramifications was written by Kopels and Kagle (1993).

Child Abuse

Estimates are that over one million American children are being subjected to abuse and neglect at any given time (Crime Prevention Center, 1988). It is therefore reasonable to assume that clinical social workers will be confronted with suspicions of child abuse among the families they see. Reporting child abuse is moral, just, and lifesaving. The purpose is clear—save children from emotional and physical trauma or death. The 1974 National Child Abuse Prevention and Treatment Act (PL93-247) defines child abuse and neglect as follows:

Physical or mental injury, sexual abuse or exploitation, negligent treatment, or maltreatment of a child under the age of eighteen or the age specified by the child protection law of the state in question, by a person who is responsible for the child's welfare, under circumstances which indicate that the child's health or welfare is harmed or threatened thereby.

Every state has a *mandatory* reporting law that requires social workers and other professionals to report suspected cases of child neglect and abuse. Because reporting laws vary from state to state, practitioners must periodically check with state agencies to become familiar with their state laws. For example, each state has specific procedures regarding when, how, and to whom verbal and written reports of abuse must be filed. In California, for instance, suspected cases should be reported to child protective agencies immediately by telephone and a written report must be sent within 36 hours of discovering the incident (California Child Abuse Reporting Law, 1963).

A number of states require professionals to take continuing education workshops on child abuse assessment and reporting before they are permitted to take licensing exams or renew their current license.

Failure to report suspected abuse places clinicians at risk for fines and imprisonment. Workers can also be sued for monetary damages if they do not report. On the other hand, social workers might worry that if they make a report to the Child Protective Services (CPS) and the suspicions are found to be false, an irate parent might retaliate with a civil suit. Fortunately, workers in every state are provided with immunity from civil suits that may arise from the reporting of suspected neglect and abuse. In addition, the law does not require the social worker to investigate the situation. That is the job of the CPS or of law enforcement.

At first glance, this appears simple: A worker receives training on recognizing child abuse and neglect, he suspects an abuse situation, he obeys the mandatory laws about reporting by notifying CPS. The CPS investigates. Ultimately, the child is removed from the abusive home and placed in a foster home where he thrives. The abusive parent gets treatment, and eventually the family is reunited.

Unfortunately, real life is frequently more complex. In another example, the social worker notices that a child client has become withdrawn, has several large bruises on her legs, and complains about being mad at Daddy but won't tell why. The worker is alarmed and suspects abuse—possibly sexual abuse. He calls CPS. Up until this point, the worker had met with the family, individually and together, for six sessions. The parents had begun to talk openly about their mutual alcohol addiction, their unemployment, and the husband's depression. They had joined AA and were making progress on their goals within the context of a therapeutic relationship. Herein lies the dilemma: The worker is not certain that the youngster has been abused, although she certainly displays several classic signs. However, because he is suspicious, he follows the law and makes the report. The mother and father are infuriated. The couple feel betrayed; they believed that what happened in the session would always be confidential (even though they had read the contract regarding exceptions to confidentiality). An investigation fails to uncover abuse. Despite the social worker's efforts, the couple never returns.

Although this case did not have a happy ending, other situations do. Sometimes perpetrators of abuse are grateful to be found out, realizing it was for the welfare of the child and that someone else had to assume the responsibility when they could not.

Elder Abuse

Elder abuse has been called the "secret epidemic" (FHP Foundation, 1995). Many older Americans are silently exploited through physical, emotional, and financial abuse from families, acquaintances, and institutions. Although many cities and counties do have some type of adult protective services, there is no mandated reporting for *suspected* abuse, nor any standardized protocol for reporting, investigation, or intervention.

There is a lack of enforcement of existing laws, and there are few shelters for elderly abuse victims.

Why Do Some Social Workers I Meet Seem Not to Care?

A clinical social worker, fresh from the university, enthusiastic, idealistic, and energetic, arrives at his first job, a residence for emotionally disturbed children. He is excited about meeting the staff and the clients. After only a few months, his excitement is replaced by a nagging disappointment. Not all, but some, of his social work colleagues seem to care very little about the troubled youths at the home. He notices that these workers often arrive late for work, leave early, take extended breaks, and avoid contact with their young clients as much as possible. They display a cynical attitude about treatment, blame the kids for all their misfortune, and talk to them in a judgmental, derogatory way. They generally seem uninterested in the kids' welfare or the performance of their social work duties.

Observing such behavior is certainly demoralizing for the uninitiated as well as the veteran social worker. Why do these social workers seem not to care? They must have cared at some point. Why else would someone choose to become a social worker? The "not caring" behavior is the most observable component of an unfortunate occupational hazard called *burnout*.[7]

Causes of Burnout

Although burnout can occur in any job situation, workers in the helping professions are especially prone to it. Among the underlying causes are the following:

---

[7]There is no single definition of burnout. Freudenberger (1974) was the first to use the term to describe the emotional and physical exhaustion experienced by workers in an institutional setting. Later, Maslach (1986) defined it as "a syndrome of emotional exhaustion, depersonalization, and reduced personal accomplishment that can occur among individuals who work with people in some capacity" (p. 182). The physical component includes chronic fatigue, weakness, accident proneness, susceptibility to illness, nausea, and muscle tension (Pines, Aronson, & Kafry, 1981).

- Individual personality characteristics (e.g., overly anxious individuals who are self-punitive when they fail to achieve their unrealistic high goals [Cherniss, 1980]).

- Alienation, a condition in which individuals experience themselves and significant aspects of the physical and social environment as estranged and out of their control (Keefe, 1984; Powell, 1994).

- Overinvolvement or excessive commitment to clients, which may be detrimental to client, social worker, or both (Koeske & Kelly, 1995).

- System factors. The initial literature on burnout conceptualized it as an *individual* inability to cope with work stresses. Thus, subsequent remedies focused on the individual (Powell, 1994). Later, authors shifted this focus to the *relationship between the worker and the work environment* (Arches, 1991; Cherniss, 1980; Hartman, 1991; Karger, 1981; Paine, 1982; Walsh, 1987).

Some level of burnout may be inevitable for all human service workers (Edelwich & Brodsky, 1983; Leitner, 1991). Thus, clinical social workers and their supervisors need to be alert to the symptoms and take early action for self-treatment.

Techniques for Prevention of and Coping With the Stresses That Contribute to the Burnout Syndrome

- Undergo personal therapy (Watkins, 1983).

- Associate with well-adjusted, healthy individuals (Watkins, 1983).

- Schedule an unwinding activity between work and home, such as jogging, listening to music, walking, or meditation (Pines et al., 1981).

- Nurture and develop close, supportive interpersonal relationships that will help buffer the effects of stress (Ratliff, 1988).

- Focus on successes rather than failures (Edelwich & Brodsky, 1983).
- Set realistic therapeutic goals. Carefully assess whether a situation is controllable or uncontrollable. If uncontrollable, focus on developing tolerance and acceptance (Folkman, 1984).
- Overcome the habit of working constantly (Oats, 1971).
- Join or form a peer group for clinicians where you can ventilate and be supported.

What Should Clinical Social Workers Know About Whistle-Blowing?

Social workers, along with other professionals, are sometimes confronted with the unethical or incompetent behavior of one of their colleagues. "Whistle-blowing" is defined as an action that is designed to bring a sharp conclusion to an activity. It usually involves informing on a person or exposing an irregularity or crime (Simpson & Weiner, 1989, p. 258). Reporting wrongdoing in the workplace has always been difficult, whether one is employed in a supermarket, a school, or a bank. Disclosing unethical or illegal practices in the workplace is a rather recent phenomenon because in the past whistle-blowing was seen as the negative action of "turncoats," "traitors," and "scabs." The whistle-blower risked being treated like an outcast (Peters & Branch, 1972). In the 1990s, however, the courage of whistle-blowers and the complexities of their actions are more appreciated (Tammelleo, 1990).

Glazer and Glazer (1989) suggest replacing the old term, with its negative connotations, with the newer term "ethical resisters" to denote "commitment to...honesty, individual responsibility, and active concern for the public good" (p. 4). The NASW, in its Code of Ethics, urges social workers to take appropriate steps in dealing with incompetent or unethical behavior:

The social worker should take action through appropriate channels against unethical conduct by any member of the profession. (NASW, 1993b; see Appendix)

Regrettably, some social workers may neglect their duties or engage in misconduct or unethical practices. In this regard, they are no different from lawyers, physicians, or nurses who are not performing their duties as they should. Nevertheless, whistle-blowing is replete with risk—for example, losing one's job or jeopardizing one's future career.

In essence, the whistle-blowing dilemma is a value dilemma; one has to weigh what is most important. For example, should one:

- Maintain the status quo and thus protect one's economic well-being and avoid incurring a reputation for being a troublemaker (although this does not come without emotional cost)?
- Remain "loyal" by being silent, thus protecting an otherwise good institution from negative public attention?
- Take action and thus protect the health and well-being of clients or patients?

Practitioners should never act impulsively but should anticipate the ramifications of their actions. Above all, clinicians should consult with others who have had personal experience and should follow these guidelines:

- Write a summary of the situation, including the source of the information, dates, times, circumstances of particular events and why they are significant, and what should be done. Meticulous documentation is important at every stage.
- Focus on making your disclosure as objective as possible. Name-calling and personal accusations will weaken your case and put you at risk for a libel or slander lawsuit.

- Try to obtain verification from other professionals.
- Always attempt to correct the situation internally first, using the internal chain of command, before contacting outside regulatory agencies.
- Prepare yourself for retaliation. Document evidence of retaliation.
- Anticipate a long haul. These issues do not get resolved quickly.
- Know when to move on. With or without resolution, the workplace may continue to be inhospitable to you (Raven-Hansen, 1980).

What Should I Know About Testifying in Court?

"Sooner or later...nearly every social worker—regardless of agency setting—will face serving as a witness" (Sheafor et al., 1994, p. 163) or will have a client's record subpoenaed. "Nearly every" seems a lot, but I would agree that the chances of appearing in court sometime during one's career are high. Clinical social workers must thus understand that a client's right to confidentiality does not necessarily extend into a court of law. Perlman (1988) writes: "The first general principle of social work confidentiality is that nothing about the subject can be chiseled in stone" (p. 425).

Although states increasingly have granted social workers the protection of *privileged communication*—"the premise and understanding between a professional person and client will not be divulged to others without express permission" (Barker, 1991, p. 182)— many states still have not. Privilege belongs to the client; under privilege, social workers may not reveal information to the court without the informed consent of the client. Therefore, if a social worker is called to the stand, her client's attorney could invoke the privilege to prohibit testimony of the practitioner (Bernstein, 1977). On the other hand, if—in a court's judgment—disclosure of confidential information would produce benefits that outweigh the injury that might occur by revealing that information, the judge may waive privilege (Hepworth & Larsen, 1993). This is only a small sample of possibilities. Bernstein (1977) recommends that clients should be made aware of the limits of confidentiality and privilege and be required to sign a document acknowledging their understanding. For further explication of this complex issue, read Schwartz (1989) and Perlman (1988).

Social workers may also be called upon to provide expert testimony. The law defines an individual as an expert if he or she has special knowledge, skill, experience, training, or education. Experts, once qualified by the court, may offer their expert opinions about the meaning of facts and observations and may also assist the court in understanding specialized information. The following guidelines for testifying, developed by L. M. Clark, a Santa Clara (Calif.) County Deputy County Counsel, were listed in the *NASW California News* (Clark, 1993):

- Always tell the truth.
- Be calm, sincere, and professionally detached, especially when challenged or criticized.
- Dress as you would for a job interview.
- Listen carefully to each question, pause, think, then respond directly to the question asked.
- Never answer a question that you do not understand.
- Never respond until the question is completed.
- Never guess or speculate. You are not required to offer an opinion on something that is speculative.
- Avoid professional jargon.
- Offer to explain your answer if necessary.
- If you don't understand a question, ask that it be rephrased.
- Never attempt to evade a question.
- Never argue with the court or a lawyer.
- Always show respect for everyone in the courtroom.
- Stop talking when an objection is made.
- Avoid humor or sarcasm.

- Do not convey with your body what you would not convey with your mouth.
- Avoid mitigating phrases like "I think" or "I suppose" or "It seemed."
- Always be thoroughly organized and prepared.
- Notes are permissible.
- You are entitled to compensation (at your customary hourly fee) for the time you spent testifying (Shapiro, 1994, p. 8).

Is It Okay to Advertise Social Work Services?

At one time, advertising of mental health services (by psychiatrists, psychologists, social workers, etc.) was considered unethical and unprofessional. However, that is no longer the case. The NASW Code of Ethics (NASW, 1993b; see Appendix B) does not forbid advertisement. It states only that "the social worker should make no misrepresentation in advertising as to qualifications, competence, service, or results to be achieved." Independent practitioners use advertising as an effective marketing tool to promote their practice. Both private and public social service agencies and institutions are using tasteful ads to market their specialized services. This is especially true in the areas of substance abuse, eating disorders, and adolescent and adult depression.

How Does Managed Care Affect Me as a Clinical Social Worker?

Managed care (MC) is a term used to signify organized health and mental health care programs designed to provide low-cost, high-quality treatment. The managed care industry changes so rapidly that the information on these pages may be obsolete before this book reaches you.

Although MC programs vary considerably in the benefits they offer, they share one common feature—the *gatekeeper*. The gatekeeper or case manager (who is a social worker, psychologist, or psychiatrist) receives information about the case from the clinician (service provider). The case manager, in turn, determines the amount and type of services that the consumer will receive. He or she also monitors the way in which benefits are dispersed. A client has only a limited amount of service benefits. If a client's problem is chronic, the case manager may decide that it is best not to use all of the benefits for the current mental health crisis. The remaining benefits may be held in reserve for later crises. For example, if a client is still extremely anxious after a period of time deemed adequate to reduce anxiety, the case manager may challenge the provider's treatment.

Social workers have a variety of roles in managed care; besides being case managers, they may be executives, administrators, and utilization management staff. They can also be found in leadership capacities, helping to develop new managed care models. *Clinical* social workers, in particular, are well represented as direct providers of services, working under contract to managed care organizations.

The present managed care market has made mental health care available to more people. Individuals who would probably not seek counseling from independent professionals are comfortable using their MC benefit for short-term mental health services. However, there are several concerns about managed care. Treatment is limited. This is acceptable for minor disorders and problems in living. However, the patient who has a more serious characterological disorder or persistent mental illness also receives a limited number of sessions. In such cases, clinical social workers may find themselves advocating, for example, for more sessions for a client who refuses medication, while the case manager allows only a limited number of sessions plus psychotropic medications monitored by a psychiatrist.

Clinicians complain bitterly about the paperwork. Many MCs are planning to go on-line so that service providers will have the capacity to make their frequent reports in response to "prompts" on their telephone line or computer screen. Of course, computerized records open new concerns about the sanctity of confidentiality in managed care organizations.

Many practitioners are finding it difficult to maintain independent practices in this new environment. The result is that many are forming group practices, where they enjoy centralized billing arrangements. These group practices are usually composed of clinicians with an array of complementary specializations to attract additional MC contracts. According to the NASW:

Social workers who provide treatment under managed systems need to refine the skills necessary to work within this environment. The ability to clearly articulate client needs, treatment plans, outcome data, and a clearly defined specialty substantiated with documentation of training and continuing education are now vital components of outpatient practice...Business skills, such as the gathering and use of marketing data and contract pricing, are now important components of any provider system. (NASW National Council on the Practice of Clinical Social Work, 1993, pp. 8–9)

Managed Care organizations are highly competitive, each trying to manage costs while maintaining or improving quality of care. The rationale for the encouragement of managed care organizations is that they are supposed to curtail the rapid escalation of health care costs in the United States. They have been held out by the Federal administration as the solution to America's failing health care system.[8]

---

[8]Over 37 million Americans are without any health care insurance coverage. The high cost of health care is unacceptable to individuals, businesses, and every level of government. The quality of care varies from the best in the world to inadequate, often depending on the economic level of the consumer (NASW, 1993a).

APPENDIX A

RECOMMENDED READINGS

Many of the books I have recommended here are fairly recent discoveries—books I have used with success in the classroom and books that have informed my teaching. Others have been around for some time but still are as fresh and relevant as the day they were published. Together, they provide a basic foundation for clinical social work.

Assessment

Fischer, J. M., & Corcoran, K. (1994). *Measures for clinical practice* (2nd ed.). *Vol. 1: Couples, families and children. Vol. 2: Adults.* New York: The Free Press.

Karls, J. M., & Wandrei, K. E. (Eds.). (1994). *Person-in-environment system: The Pie classification system for social functioning problems.* Washington, DC: National Association of Social Workers. (This book illustrates the use of a newly developed classification system for social work practice.)

Lukas, S. (1993). *Where to start & what to ask: An assessment handbook.* New York: W. W. Norton.

Mattaini, M. A. (1993). *More than a thousand words: Graphics for clinical practice.* Washington, DC: National Association of Social Workers.

Morrison, J. M. (1995). *The first interview* (rev. for DSM-IV). New York: Guilford Press.

Shulman, L. (1992). *The skills of helping individuals, families, and groups* (3rd ed.). Itasca, IL: F. E. Peacock.

Couples and Families

Griffin, W. A. (1993). *Family therapy: Fundamentals of theory and practice*. New York: Brunner/Mazel.

Hartman, A., & Laird, J. (1983). *Family centered social work practice*. New York: The Free Press.

Jacobson, N. S., & Margolin, G. (1979). *Marital therapy: Strategies and behavior exchange principles*. New York: Brunner/ Mazel. (A behavioral approach)

Kaplan, L., & Girard, J. L. (1994). *Strengthening high-risk families: A handbook for practitioners*. New York: Lexington Books.

McKerry, P. C., & Price, S. J. (1994). *Families & change: Coping with stressful events*. Thousand Oaks, CA: Sage.

Minuchin, S., & Fishman, H. C. (1981). *Family therapy techniques*. Cambridge, MA: Harvard University Press.

Groups

Bernard, H. S., & MacKenzie, K. R. (Eds.). (1994). *Basics of group therapy*. New York: Guilford Press.

Lonergan, E. C. (1989). *Group intervention: How to begin and maintain groups in medical and psychiatric settings*. New York: Jason Aronson.

Reid, K. L. (1991). *Social work practice with groups: A clinical perspective*. Pacific Grove, CA: Brooks/Cole.

Rose, S. D., & Edleson, J. L. (1987). *Working with children and adolescents in groups*. San Francisco: Jossey-Bass.

Yalom, I. D. (1983). *Inpatient group psychotherapy*. New York: Basic Books. (Group work in acute psychiatric settings)

Yalom, I. D. (1985). *The theory and practice of group psychotherapy* (3rd ed.). New York: Basic Books.

Models

The following books focus on one or more treatment models commonly used in clinical social work practice.

Dorfman, R. A. (Ed.). (1988). *Paradigms of clinical social work.* New York: Brunner/Mazel.

Fisher, D. D. V. (1991). *An introduction to constructivism for social workers.* New York: Praeger.

Goldstein, E. G. (1995). *Ego psychology and social work practice* (2nd ed.). New York: The Free Press.

Meyer, C. H. (Ed.). (1983). *Clinical social work in the eco-systems perspective.* New York: Columbia University Press.

Rothman, J. (1994). *Practice with highly vulnerable clients: Case management and community-based services.* Englewood Cliffs, NJ: Prentice Hall.

Saari, C. (1991). *The creation of meaning in social work.* New York: Guilford Press.

Strean, H. S. (1994). *Essentials of psychoanalysis.* New York: Brunner/Mazel.

Turner, F. J. (1986). *Social work treatment: Interlocking theoretical approaches* (3rd ed.). New York: The Free Press.

Wells, R. A. (1994). *Planned short-term treatment* (2nd ed.). New York: The Free Press.

Diversity

Ho, M. K. (1987). *Family therapy with ethnic minorities.* Newbury Park, CA: Sage.

McGoldrick, M., Pearce, J. K., & Giordano, J. (Eds.). (1987). *Ethnicity and family therapy.* New York: Guilford Press.

Pinderhughes, E. (1989). *Understanding race, ethnicity, and power: The key to efficacy in clinical practice.* New York: The Free Press.

Saba, G. W., Karrer, B. M., & Hardy, K. V. (Eds.). (1990). *Minorities and family therapy.* New York: Haworth Press.

Sue, D. W., & Sue, D. (1990). *Counseling the culturally different: Theory and practice* (2nd ed.). New York: John Wiley.

Clinical Social Work Research

Blythe, B., Tripodi, T., & Briar, S. (1994). *Direct practice research in human service agencies.* New York: Columbia University Press.

Royce, D. (1992). *Research methods in social work.* Chicago: Nelson-Hall.

Rubin, A., & Babbie, E. (1993). *Research methods for social work.* Pacific Grove, CA: Brooks/Cole.

Tripodi, T. (1994). *A primer on single-subject design for clinical social workers.* Washington, DC: NASW Press.

APPENDIX B

THE NASW CODE OF ETHICS[1]

I. **The Social Worker's Conduct and Comportment as a Social Worker**

   A. *Propriety—The social worker should maintain high standards of personal conduct in the capacity or identity as social worker.*

   1. The private conduct of the social worker is a personal matter to the same degree as is any other person's, except when such conduct compromises the fulfillment of professional responsibilities.
   2. The social worker should not participate in, condone, or be associated with dishonesty, fraud, deceit, or misrepresentation.
   3. The social worker should distinguish clearly be-

---

[1]National Association of Social Workers. (1993b). Code of Ethics of the National Association of Social Workers. Washington, DC: Author. Reprinted by permission.

tween statements and actions made as a private individual and as a representative of the social work profession or an organization or group.

B. *Competence and Professional Development—The social worker should strive to become and remain proficient in professional practice and the performance of professional functions.*

1. The social worker should accept responsibility or employment only on the basis of existing competence or the intention to acquire the necessary competence.
2. The social worker should not misrepresent professional qualifications, education, experience, or affiliations.
3. The social worker should not allow his or her own personal problems, psychosocial distress, substance abuse, or mental health difficulties to interfere with professional judgment and performance or jeopardize the best interests of those for whom the social worker has a professional responsibility.
4. The social worker whose personal problems, psychosocial distress, substance abuse, or mental health difficulties interfere with professional judgment and performance should immediately seek consultation and take appropriate remedial action by seeking professional help, making adjustments in workload, terminating practice, or taking any other steps necessary to protect clients and others.

C. *Service—The social worker should regard as primary the service obligation of the social work profession.*

1. The social worker should retain ultimate responsibility for the quality and extent of the service that individual assumes, assigns, or performs.
2. The social worker should act to prevent practices

that are inhumane or discriminatory against any
person or group of persons.

D. *Integrity—The social worker should act in accor-*
    dance with the highest standards of professional
    integrity and impartiality.

    1. The social worker should be alert to and resist the
        influences and pressures that interfere with the
        exercise of professional discretion and impartial
        judgment required for the performance of profes-
        sional functions.
    2. The social worker should not exploit professional
        relationships for personal gain.

E. *Scholarship and Research—The social worker en-*
    gaged in study and research should be guided by the
    conventions of scholarly inquiry.

    1. The social worker engaged in research should
        consider carefully its possible consequences for
        human beings.
    2. The social worker engaged in research should
        ascertain that the consent of participants in the
        research is voluntary and informed, without any
        implied deprivation or penalty for refusal to par-
        ticipate, and with due regard for participants' pri-
        vacy and dignity.
    3. The social worker engaged in research should
        protect participants from unwarranted physical
        or mental discomfort, distress, harm, danger, or
        deprivation.
    4. The social worker who engages in the evaluation of
        services or cases should discuss them only for the
        professional purposes and only with persons di-
        rectly and professionally concerned with them.
    5. Information obtained about participants in research
        should be treated as confidential.
    6. The social worker should take credit only for work

actually done in connection with scholarly and
research endeavors and credit contributions made
by others.

II. The Social Worker's Ethical Responsibility to Clients.

F. *Primacy of Clients' Interests—The social worker's primary responsibility is to clients*

1. The social worker should serve clients with devotion, loyalty, determination, and the maximum application of professional skill and competence.
2. The social worker should not exploit relationships with clients for personal advantage.
3. The social worker should not practice, condone, facilitate, or collaborate with any form of discrimination on the basis of race, color, sex, sexual orientation, age, religion, national origin, marital status, political belief, mental or physical handicap, or any other preference or personal characteristic, condition, or status.
4. The social worker should not condone or engage in any dual or multiple relationships with clients or former clients in which there is a risk of exploitation of or potential harm to the client. The social worker is responsible for setting clear, appropriate, and culturally sensitive boundaries.
5. The social worker should under no circumstances engage in sexual activities with clients.
6. The social worker should provide clients with accurate and complete information regarding the extent and nature of the services available to them.
7. The social worker should apprise clients of their risks, rights, opportunities, and obligations associated with social service to them.
8. The social worker should seek advice and counsel of colleagues and supervisors whenever such consultation is in the best interest of clients.

9. The social worker should terminate service to clients, and professional relationships with them, when such service and relationships are no longer required or no longer serve the clients' needs or interests.

10. The social worker should withdraw services precipitously only under unusual circumstances, giving careful consideration to all factors in the situation and taking care to minimize possible adverse effects.

11. The social worker who anticipates the termination or interruption of service to clients should notify clients promptly and seek the transfer, referral, or continuation of service in relation to the clients' needs and preferences.

G. *Rights and Prerogatives of Clients—The social worker should make every effort to foster maximum self-determination on the part of clients.*

1. When the social worker must act on behalf of a client who has been adjudged legally incompetent, the social worker should safeguard the interests and rights of that client.

2. When another individual has been legally authorized to act in behalf of a client, the social worker should deal with that person always with the client's best interest in mind.

3. The social worker should not engage in any action that violates or diminishes the civil or legal rights of clients.

H. *Confidentiality and Privacy—The social worker should respect the privacy of clients and hold in confidence all information obtained in the course of professional service.*

1. The social worker should share with others confi-

dences revealed by clients, without their consent, only for compelling professional reasons.

2. The social worker should inform clients fully about the limits of confidentiality in a given situation, the purposes for which information is obtained, and how it may be used.

3. The social worker should afford clients reasonable access to any official social work records concerning them.

4. When providing clients with access to records, the social worker should take due care to protect the confidences of others contained in those records.

5. The social worker should obtain informed consent of clients before taping, recording, or permitting third party observation of their activities.

I. *Fees—When setting fees, the social worker should ensure that they are fair, reasonable, considerate, and commensurate with the service performed and with due regard for the clients' ability to pay.*

1. The social worker should not accept anything of value for making a referral.

III. The Social Worker's Ethical Responsibility to Colleagues

J. *Respect, Fairness, and Courtesy—The social worker should treat colleagues with respect, courtesy, fairness, and good faith.*

1. The social worker should cooperate with colleagues to promote professional interests and concerns.

2. The social worker should respect confidences shared by colleagues in the course of their professional relationships and transactions.

3. The social worker should create and maintain conditions of practice that facilitate ethical and competent professional performance by colleagues.

4. The social worker should treat with respect, and represent accurately and fairly, the qualifications,

views, and findings of colleagues and use appropriate channels to express judgments on these matters.

5. The social worker who replaces or is replaced by a colleague in professional practice should act with consideration for the interest, character, and reputation of that colleague.

6. The social worker should not exploit a dispute between a colleague and employers to obtain a position or otherwise advance the social worker's interest.

7. The social worker should seek arbitration or mediation when conflicts with colleagues require resolution for compelling professional reasons.

8. The social worker should extend to colleagues of other professions the same respect and cooperation that is extended to social work colleagues.

9. The social worker who serves as an employer, supervisor, or mentor to colleagues should make orderly and explicit arrangements regarding the conditions of their continuing professional relationship.

10. The social worker who has the responsibility for employing and evaluating the performance of other staff members should fulfill such responsibility in a fair, considerate, and equitable manner, on the basis of clearly enunciated criteria.

11. The social worker who has the responsibility for evaluating the performance of employees, supervisees, or students should share evaluations with them.

12. The social worker should not use a professional position vested with power, such as that of employer, supervisor, teacher, or consultant, to his or her advantage or to exploit others.

13. The social worker who has direct knowledge of a social work colleague's impairment due to personal problems, psychosocial distress, substance abuse, or mental health difficulties should consult

with that colleague and assist the colleague in taking remedial action.

K. *Dealing with Colleagues' Clients—The social worker has the responsibility to relate to the clients of colleagues with full professional consideration.*

1. The social worker should not assume professional responsibility for the clients of another agency or a colleague without appropriate communication with that agency or colleague.
2. The social worker who serves the clients of colleagues, during a temporary absence or emergency, should serve those clients with the same consideration as that afforded any client.

IV. **The Social Worker's Ethical Responsibility to Employers and Employing Organizations**

L. *Commitments to Employing Organizations—The social worker should adhere to commitments made to the employing organization.*

1. The social worker should work to improve the employing agency's policies and procedures and the efficiency and effectiveness of its services.
2. The social worker should not accept employment or arrange student field placements in an organization which is currently under public sanction by NASW for violating personnel standards, or imposing limitations on or penalties for professional actions on behalf of clients.
3. The social worker should act to prevent and eliminate discrimination in the employing organization's work assignments and in its employment policies and practices.
4. The social worker should use with scrupulous regard, and only for the purpose for which they are intended, the resources of the employing organization.

V. The Social Worker's Ethical Responsibility to the Social Work Profession

M. Mandating the Integrity of the Profession—The social worker should uphold and advance the values, ethics, knowledge, and mission of the profession.

1. The social worker should protect and enhance the dignity and integrity of the profession and should be responsible and vigorous in discussion and criticism of the profession.
2. The social worker should take action through appropriate channels against unethical conduct by any other member of the profession.
3. The social worker should act to prevent the unauthorized and unqualified practice of social work.
4. The social worker should make no misrepresentation in advertising as to qualifications, competence, service, or results to be achieved.

N. Community Service—The social worker should assist the profession in making social services available to the general public.

1. The social worker should contribute time and professional expertise to activities that promote respect for the utility, the integrity, and the competence of the social work profession.
2. The social worker should support the formulation, development, enactment, and implementation of social policies of concern to the profession.

O. Development of Knowledge—The social worker should take responsibility for identifying, developing, and fully utilizing knowledge for professional practice.

1. The social worker should base practice upon recognized knowledge relevant to social work.
2. The social worker should critically examine and

keep current with emerging knowledge relevant to
social work.

3. The social worker should contribute to the knowl-
    edge base of social work and share research knowl-
    edge and practice wisdom with colleagues.

VI. The Social Worker's Ethical Responsibility to Society

P. *Promoting the General Welfare—The social worker should promote the general welfare of society.*

1. The social worker should act to prevent and elimi-
    nate discrimination against any person or group on
    the basis of race, color, sex, sexual orientation, age,
    religion, national origin, marital status, political
    belief, mental or physical handicap, or any other
    preference or personal characteristic, condition, or
    status.

2. The social worker should act to ensure that all
    persons have access to the resources, services, and
    opportunities which they require.

3. The social worker should act to expand choice and
    opportunity for all persons, with special regard for
    disadvantaged or oppressed groups and persons.

4. The social worker should promote conditions that
    encourage respect for the diversity of cultures
    which constitute American society.

5. The social worker should provide appropriate pro-
    fessional services in public emergencies.

6. The social worker should advocate changes in
    policy and legislation to improve social conditions
    and to promote social justice.

7. The social worker should encourage informed par-
    ticipation by the public in shaping social policies
    and institutions.

REFERENCES

Applebaum, P. S., & Jorgenson, L. (1991). Psychotherapist–patient sexual contact after termination of treatment: An analysis and a proposal. *American Journal of Psychiatry*, *148*(11), 1466–1473.

Arches, J. (1991). Social structure, burnout, and job satisfaction. *Social Work*, *36*, 202–206.

Bandler, B. (1963). The concept of ego-supportive psychotherapy. In H. Parad & R. Miller (Eds.), *Ego-oriented casework* (pp. 27–44). New York: Family Service Association of America.

Barker, R. L. (1991). *The social work dictionary* (2nd ed.). Silver Spring, MD: National Association of Social Workers.

Barlow, D. H., & Hersen, M. (1984). *Single case experimental designs: Strategies for studying behavior change* (2nd ed.). New York: Pergamon Press.

Bergman, A. S., Contro, N. H., & Zivetz, N. (1984). Clinical social work in a medical setting. *Social Work in Health Care*, *9*(3), 1–11.

Bernstein, B. (1977). Privileged communications to the social worker. *Social Work*, *22*, 264–268.

Bloom, M. (1983). Empirically based clinical research. In A.

Rosenblatt & D. Waldfogel (Eds.), *Handbook of clinical social work* (pp. 560–582). San Francisco: Jossey-Bass.

Bloom, M., Fischer, J., & Orme, J. (1995). *Evaluating practice: Guidelines for the accountable professional* (2nd ed.). Needham Heights, MA: Allyn & Bacon.

Blythe, B. J., & Briar, S. (1985). Developing empirically based models of practice. *Social Work, 30,* 483–488.

Blythe, B., & Tripodi, T. (1989). *Measurement in direct social work practice.* Newbury Park, CA: Sage.

Blythe, B. J., Tripodi, T., & Briar, S. (1994). *Direct practice research in human service agencies.* New York: Columbia University Press.

Borys, D. (1988). *Dual relationships between therapist and client: A national survey of clinicians' attitudes and practices.* Unpublished doctoral dissertation, University of California, Los Angeles.

Bowen, M. (1978). *Family therapy in clinical practice.* New York: Jason Aronson.

Bowlby, J. (1980). *Attachment and loss, Vol. 3: Loss, sadness, and depression.* New York: Basic Books.

Boyd-Franklin, N. (1989). *Black families in therapy: A multisystems approach.* New York: Guilford Press.

Briar, S. (1973). Effective social work intervention in direct practice: Implications for education. In S. Briar, W. B. Cannon, L. H. Ginsberg, S. Horn, & R. C. Sarri (Eds.), *Facing the challenge: Plenary session from the 19th Annual Program Meeting* (pp. 17–30). New York: Council on Social Work Education.

Briar, S. (1977). Incorporating research into education for clinical practice in social work: Toward a clinical science in social work. In A. Rubin & A. Rosenblatt (Eds.), *Sourcebook on research utilization* (pp. 132–140). New York: Council on Social Work Education.

Briar, S., & Miller, H. (1971). *Problems and issues in social casework.* New York: Columbia University Press.

Bullis, R. K. (1995). *Clinical social worker misconduct: Law, ethics, and personal dynamics.* Chicago: Nelson-Hall.

Burns, D. D. (1993). *Ten days to self-esteem*. New York: Quill William Morrow.

California Child Abuse Reporting Law, penal code section 11166–11174. (1963).

California Society for Clinical Social Work. (1993).*Professional business forms for the mental health clinician: A sampler*. Sacramento, CA: Author.

Carter, B., & McGoldrick, M. (1988). *The changing family lifestyle: A framework for family therapy* (2nd ed.). Boston: Allyn & Bacon.

Cherniss, C. (1980). *Staff burnout: Job stress in human services*. Beverly Hills, CA: Sage.

Cicchitto, F. R. (1983). Countertransference reactions to forced and natural termination of psychotherapy (Doctoral dissertation, California School of Professional Psychology, 1983). *Dissertation Abstracts International, 43*, 3727B–3728B.

Clark, L. M. (1993, November). [Guidelines for testifying in court.] Cited by P. A. Merek, *NASW California News*, p. 12.

Corey, G., Corey, M. S., & Callanan, P. (1993). *Issues and ethics in the helping professions*. Pacific Grove, CA: Brooks/Cole.

Corsini, R. J. (Ed.). (1981). *Handbook of innovative psychotherapies*. New York: John Wiley.

Corsini, R. J., & Wedding, D. (1989). Current psychotherapies (4th ed.). Itasca, IL: F. E. Peacock.

Cowger, C. D., & Atherton, C. R. (1974). Social control: A rationale for social welfare. *Social Work, 19*(4), 456–462.

Crime Prevention Center, California Office of the Attorney General. (1988). *Child Abuse Prevention Handbook*. Sacramento: Author.

Davis, A. F. (1967). *Spearheads for reform: The social settlements and the progressive movement, 1890–1914*. New York: Oxford University Press.

Dorfman, R. A. (1987a). Adult education and group therapy. *The Journal for Specialists in Group Work, 12*(2), 65–69.

Dorfman, R. A. (1987b). Rules of thumb: Constructing guidelines for the beginning clinical social worker. *The Clinical Supervisor, 5*(4), 87–96.

Dorfman, R. A. (1988a). Clinical social work: The development of a discipline. In R. A. Dorfman (Ed.), *Paradigms of clinical social work* (pp. 3–24). New York: Brunner/Mazel.

Dorfman, R. A. (Ed.). (1988b). *Paradigms of clinical social work.* New York: Brunner/Mazel.

Dorfman, R. A., Walters, K., Burke, P., Harden, L., Karanik, T., Raphael, J., & Silverstein, E. (1995). Old, sad, and alone: The myth of the aging homosexual. *Journal of Gerontological Social Work, 24*(½),29–44.

Dubos, R. (1968). *So human an animal.* New York: Scribner.

Dubos, R. (1972). *A god within.* New York: Scribner.

Edelwich, J., & Brodsky, A. (1983). *Burn-out: Stages of disillusionment in the helping professions.* New York: Pergamon Press.

Edelwich, J., & Brodsky, A. (1991). *Sexual dilemmas for the helping professional* (rev. and expanded ed.). New York: Brunner/Mazel.

Elbow, M. (1987). The memory books: Facilitating termination with children. *Social Casework, 68,* 180–183.

Ell, K. (1984). Social networks, social support and health status: A review. *Social Service Review, 58,* 133–149.

Epstein, L. (1980). *Helping people: The task centered approach.* St. Louis, MO: C. V. Mosby Press.

FHP Foundation. (1995). *Silent suffering: Elder abuse in America* (report on focus group activities and recommendations for the 1995 White House conference on aging). Long Beach, CA: Author.

Fischer, J. (1973). Is casework effective? *Social Work, 18,* 5–20.

Fischer, J. (1978). *Effective casework practice: An eclectic approach.* New York: McGraw-Hill.

Fischer, J., & Corcoran, K. (1994). *Measures for clinical practice* (2nd ed.). New York: The Free Press.

Flexner, A. (1915). Is social work a profession? *Proceedings of the National Conference of Charities and Correction.* Chicago: The Conference.

Folkman, S. (1984). Personal control and stress coping processes: A theoretical analysis. *Journal of Personality and Social Psychology, 46*(4), 839–852.

Fortune, A. E., Pearlingi, B., & Rochelle, C. D. (1992). Reactions to termination of individual treatment. *Social Work, 37*(2), 171–178.

Fox, R. (1989). What is meta for? *Clinical Social Work Journal, 17*(3), 233–244.

Freedberg, S. M., & Goldstein, J. L. (1986). Bertha Capin Reynolds. In W. I. Trattner (Ed.), *Biographical dictionary of social welfare in America.* New York: Greenwood Press.

Freud, S. (1963). *Three case histories* (P. Rieff, Ed.). New York: Collier Books.

Freudenberger, H. J. (1974). Staff burnout. *Journal of Social Issues, 30*(1), 159–164.

Fulero, S. M. (1988). Tarasoff: 10 years later. *Professional Psychology: Research and Practice,* (2), 184–190.

Gareffa, D. N., & Neff, S. A. (1974). Management of the client's seductive behavior. *Smith College Studies in Social Work, 44*(2), 110–124.

Garland, J. A., Jones, H. E., & Kolodny, R. L. (1973). A model for stages of development in social work groups. In S. Bernstein (Ed.), *Explorations in group work: Essays in theory and practice.* Boston: Milford House.

Geertz, C. (1987). *Words and lives: The anthropologist as author.* Stanford, CA: Stanford University Press.

Gelfand, D. E., & Fandetti, D. V. (1986). The emergent nature of ethnicity: Dilemmas in assessment. *Social Casework,* November, 542–550.

Germain, C. (1970). Casework and science: A historical encounter. In R. W. Roberts & R. H. Nee (Eds.), *Theories of social casework* (pp. 3–32). Chicago: The University of Chicago Press.

Germain, C. B., & Gitterman, A. (1986). The life model approach to social work practice revisited. In F. J. Turner (Ed.), *Social work treatment* (3rd ed., pp. 618–644). New York: The Free Press.

Gerson, R., & McGoldrick, M. (1985). The computerized genogram. *Primary Care, 12*(3), 535–545.

Girard, L. W. (1991). *Alex, the kid with AIDS.* Morton Grove, IL: Albert Whitman.

Gladow, N. W., & Pecora, P. J. (1992). Homebuilders: Helping families stay together. In C. W. Le Croy (Ed.), *Case studies in social work practice* (pp. 74–86). Belmont, CA: Wadsworth.

Glazer, M. P., & Glazer, P. M. (1989). *The whistle-blowers: Exposing corruption in government and industry.* New York: Basic Books.

Golan, N. (1978). *Treatment in crisis situations.* New York: The Free Press.

Goldwaite, D. E. (1986). The client's perspective on forced termination of psychotherapy (Doctoral dissertation, Boston College, 1985). *Dissertation Abstracts International, 47,* 2164B.

Gottesfeld, M. L., & Pharis, M. E. (1977). *Profiles in social work.* New York: Human Services Press.

Greenberg, S. (1986). The supportive approach to therapy. *Clinical Social Work Journal, 14*(1), 6–13.

Griffin, W. A. (1993). Family therapy: Fundamentals of theory and practice. New York: Brunner/Mazel.

Hamilton, G. (1940). *Theory and practice of social case work.* New York: Columbia University Press.

Hamilton, G. (1941). The underlying philosophy of social casework. *The Family, 18* (July), 139–148.

Hancock, B. L., & Pelton, L. H. (1989). Home visits: History and functions. *Social Casework,* January, 21–27.

Hartman, A. (1978). Diagrammatic assessment of family relationships. *Social Casework, 59,* 465–476.

Hartman, A. (1991). Social worker-in-situation. *Social Work, 36*(3), 195–196.

Hartman, A., & Laird, J. (1983). *Family centered social work practice.* New York: The Free Press.

Hartman, A., & Laird, J. (1985). *A handbook of child welfare: Context, knowledge, and practice.* New York: The Free Press.

Haselkorn, F. (1978). Accountability in clinical practice. *Social Casework, 59*(6), 330–336.

Hepworth, D. H., & Larsen, J. (1993). *Direct social work practice: Theory and skills* (4th ed.). Pacific Grove, CA: Brooks/Cole.

Herlihy, B., & Corey, G. (1992). *Dual relationships in counseling.* Alexandria, VA: American Counseling Association.

Hersen, M., & Bellack, A. S. (1981). *Behavioral assessment: A practical handbook* (2nd ed.). New York: Pergamon Press.

Ho, M. K. (1987). *Family therapy with ethnic minorities.* Newbury Park, CA: Sage.

Hollis, F. (1964). *Casework: A psychosocial therapy.* New York: Random House.

Hollis, F. (1972). *Casework: A psychosocial therapy* (2nd ed.). New York: Random House.

Hopke, W. E. (Ed.). (1990). *Encyclopedia of careers and vocational guidance, Vol. 2: Professional careers.* Chicago: J. G. Ferguson.

Ingersoll-Dayton, B., & Arndt, B. (1990). Uses of the genogram with the elderly and their families. *Journal of Gerontological Social Work, 15*(1/2), 105–119.

Jayaratne, S. (1982). Characteristics and theoretical orientations of clinical social workers: A national survey. *Journal of Social Service Research, 4*(2), 17–30.

Jayaratne, S. (1990). Clinical significance: Problems and new developments. In L. Videka-Sherman & W. J. Reid (Eds.), *Advances in clinical social work research* (pp. 271–285). Silver Spring, MD: NASW Press.

Jayaratne, S., & Levy, R. (1979). *Empirical clinical practice.* New York: Columbia University Press.

Jennings, M. (1990). Community mobilization. Presentation made to the National Association of Rural Mental Health Workers, Lubbock, TX. Cited in J. Hefferman, G. Shuttlesworth, & R. Ambrosino, (1992). *Social work and social welfare: An introduction* (2nd ed.). New York: West.

Kaplan, S. G., & Wheeler, E. G. (1983). Survival skills for working with potentially violent clients. *Social Casework, 64*, 339–346.

Karger, H. (1981). Burnout as alienation. *Social Service Review, 55*, 270–283.

Kasius, C. (1950). *A comparison of diagnostic and functional casework concepts: Report of the Family Service Association of America Committee to Study Basic Concepts in Basic Casework Practice.* New York: Family Service Association of America.

Kazdin, A. E. (1982). *Single-case research designs: Methods for clinical and applied settings.* New York: Oxford University Press.

Keefe, T. (1984). Alienation and social work practice. *Social Casework, 65,* 145–153.

Keith, C. (1966). Multiple transfers of psychotherapy patients. *Archives of General Psychiatry, 14,* 185–189.

Kirk, S., Osmalov, M., & Fischer, J. (1976). Social workers' involvement in research. *Social Work, 21*(2), 121–131.

Kluckhohn, C. (1951). Values and value orientations in the theory of action. In T. Parsons & E. A. Shils (Eds.), *Toward a general theory of action* (pp. 388–433). Cambridge, MA: Harvard University Press.

Koeske, G. F., & Kelly, T. (1995). The impact of overinvolvement on burnout and job satisfaction. *American Journal of Orthopsychiatry, 65*(2), 282–292.

Kopels, S., & Kagle, J. D. (1993). Do social workers have a duty to warn? *Social Service Review, 67*(1), 101–126.

Kopp, S. B. (1976). *If you meet a Buddha on the road, kill him!* New York: Bantam Books.

Landau-Stanton, J. (1990). Issues and methods of treatment for families in cultural transition. In M. Mirkin (Ed.), *The social and political contexts of family therapy* (pp. 251–275). Boston: Allyn & Bacon.

Lazarus, R. S. (1971). *Personality* (2nd ed.). Englewood Cliffs, NJ: Prentice-Hall.

Lefrancois, G. R. (1993). *The lifespan* (4th ed.). Belmont, CA: Wadsworth.

Leikind, B. (1995, January). *The physics of ballet.* Presented at the meeting of the Southern California Skeptics Society at Occidental College, Glendora, CA.

Leitner, M. (1991). The dream denied: Professional burnout and the constraints of human service organizations. *Canadian Psychology, 32*(4), 547–558.

Levinson, H. L. (1977). Termination of psychotherapy. Some salient issues. *Social Casework, 58,* 480–489.

Lewin, K. (1951). *Field theory in social science.* New York: Harper & Row.

Livingston, C. (1993). *Why was I adopted?* Secaucus, NJ: Carol.

Maki, M. T., Inglehart, A. P., Nakamura, C., & Nunn, J. A. (1994).

Los Angeles civil unrest: An interorganization response to crisis. *Crisis Intervention, 1*(3), 191–202.

Maslach, C. (1986). Burnout and alcoholism. In R. R. Kilburg, P. E. Nathan, & R. W. Thoreson (Eds.), *Professions in distress: Issues, syndromes and solutions in psychology* (pp. 53–75). Washington, DC: American Psychological Association.

Mayle, P., & Robins, R. (1988). *Why are we getting a divorce?* New York: Harmony Press.

McGoldrick, M. (1985). *You can go home again.* New York: W. W. Norton.

McGoldrick, M. (1991). Life connections: Family, community and culture. *Smith College School for Social Work Journal,* Fall/Winter, pp. 4–9.

McGoldrick, M., & Gerson, R. (1985). *Genograms in family assessment.* New York: W. W. Norton.

McGoldrick, M., Pearce, J., & Giordano, J. (1982). *Ethnicity and family therapy.* New York: Guilford Press.

Messer, S. B. (1986). Eclecticism in psychotherapy: Underlying assumptions, problems and tradeoffs. In J. C. Norcross (Ed.), *Handbook of eclectic psychotherapy* (pp. 379–397) New York: Brunner/Mazel.

Meyer, C. H. (1970). *Social work practice: The urban crisis.* New York: The Free Press.

Meyer, C. H. (1988). The eco-systems perspective. In R. A. Dorfman (Ed.), *Paradigms of clinical social work* (pp. 275–284). New York: Brunner/Mazel.

Meyer, C. H. (1992). Social work assessment: Is there an empirical base? *Research in Social Work Practice, 2*(3), 297–303.

Minahan, A. (Ed.). (1987). Gordon Hamilton. In *Encyclopedia of social work* (18th ed., pp. 926–927). Silver Spring, MD: National Association of Social Workers.

Moreno, J. L. (1970). *Psychodrama* (3rd ed.). New York: Beacon House.

Moss, S. Z., & Moss, M. S. (1967). When a caseworker leaves an agency: The impact on worker and client. *Social Casework,* July; 433–437.

Napier, N. J. (1990). *Recreating your self: Help for adult children of dysfunctional families.* New York: W. W. Norton.

NASW (National Association of Social Workers). (1989). *NASW*

Standards for the practice of clinical social work. Washington, DC: Author.

NASW. (1990). *NASW clinical indicators for social work and psychosocial services in the acute psychiatric hospital.* Washington, DC: Author.

NASW. (1991). *Standards of practice for social work mediators.* Washington, DC: Author.

NASW. (1993a). *Choices make a difference: Careers in social work.* Washington, DC: Author.

NASW. (1993b). *Code of ethics of the National Association of Social Workers.* Washington, DC. Author.

NASW. (1994). *Social work speaks: NASW policy statements* (3rd ed.). Washington, DC: NASW Press.

NASW National Council on the Practice of Clinical Social Work. (1993). *The social work perspective on managed care for mental health and substance abuse treatment.* Washington, DC: National Association of Social Workers.

Nelson, J. (1975). Dealing with resistance in social work practice. *Social Casework, 56,* 587–592.

Newman, E., & Turem, J. (1974). The crisis of accountability. *Social Work, 19*(1), 5–16.

Noble, D. W. (1984). Progressivism. In J. P. Greene (Ed.), *Encyclopedia of American political history. Vol. III: Studies of the principal movements and ideas* (p. 992). New York: Scribner.

Norcross, J. C. (Ed.). (1986). *Handbook of eclectic psychotherapy.* New York: Brunner/Mazel.

Northen, H. (1982). *Clinical social work.* New York: Columbia University Press.

Northen, H. (1988). *Social work with groups.* New York: Columbia University Press.

Northen, H. (1995). *Clinical social work knowledge and skills* (2nd ed.). New York: Columbia University Press.

Northen, H., & Ell, K. (1990). *Families and health care: Psychosocial intervention.* New York: Aldine DeGruyter.

Nuehring, E. M., & Pascone, A. B. (1986). Single-subject evaluation: A tool for quality assurance. *Social Work, 31,* 359–365.

Oats, W. (1971). *Confessions of a workaholic.* New York: World.

Oliner, S. T., & Oliner, P. N. (1988). *The altruistic personality: Rescuers of Jews in Nazi Europe.* New York: The Free Press.

Paine, W. S. (1982). *Job stress and burnout: Research, theory and intervention perspectives.* Beverly Hills, CA: Sage.

Palombo, J. (1982). The psychology of the self and the termination of treatment. *Clinical Social Work, 10,* 15–27.

Pelletier, K. R. (1992). *Mind as healer, mind as slayer.* New York: Dell.

Perlman, G. L. (1988). Mastering the law of privileged communication: A guide for social workers. *Social Work, 33*(5), 425–429.

Perlman, H. H. (1957). *Social casework: A problem solving approach.* Chicago: University of Chicago Press.

Perlman, H. H. (1970). The problem-solving model in social casework. In R. W. Roberts & R. H. Nee (Eds.), *Theories of social casework* (pp. 129–180). Chicago: University of Chicago Press.

Perlman, H. H. (1989). *Looking back to see ahead.* Chicago: University of Chicago Press.

Persons, J. B. (1994). Case conceptualization in cognitive-behavior therapy. In K. T. Kuehlwein & H. Rosen (Eds.), *Cognitive therapies in action: Evolving innovative practice* (pp. 33–53). San Francisco: Jossey-Bass.

Peters, C., & Branch, T. (1972). *Blowing the whistle: Dissent in the public interest.* New York: Praeger.

Phelps, J. K. (1986). *The hidden addictions and how to get free.* New York: Little, Brown.

Piaget, J. (1952). *The origins of intelligence in childhood.* New York: International Press.

Pines, A., Aronson, E., & Kafry, D. (1981). *Burn-out: From tedium to personal growth.* New York: The Free Press.

Pope, K. S., Keith-Speigel, P., & Tabachnick, B. G. (1986). Sexual attraction to clients. *American Psychologist, 41,* 147–158.

Powell, W. E. (1994). The relationship between feelings of alienation and burnout in social work. *Families in Society: The Journal of Contemporary Human Services, 75*(4), 229–235.

Rappoport, P. S. (1982). *Value for value psychotherapy: The economic and therapeutic barter.* New York: Praeger.

Ratliff, N. (1988). Stress and burnout in the helping professions. *Social Casework, 69*(3), 147–154.

Raven-Hansen, P. (1980). Dos and don'ts for whistle-blowers: Planning for trouble. *Technology Review, 82*(34), 34–44.

Reamer, F. G. (1979). Fundamental ethical issues in social work: An essay review. *Social Service Review, 53*(2), 229–243.

Red Horse, J. G. (1980). Family structure and value orientation in American Indians. *Social Casework,* October, 462–466.

Reid, W. J. (1988). Brief task-centered treatment. In R. A. Dorfman (Ed.), *Paradigms of clinical social work* (pp. 196–219). New York: Brunner/Mazel.

Reid, W. J. (1994). The empirical practice movement. *Social Service Review, 68*(2), 165–182.

Reid, W. J., & Hanrahan, P. (1982). Recent evaluations of social work: Grounds for optimism. *Social Work, 24*(4), 328–347.

Richmond, M. E. (1917). *Social diagnosis.* New York: The Free Press.

Rodman, R. (1965). *Keeping hope alive.* New York: Harper and Row.

Rosen, H. (1988). Evolving a personal philosophy of practice: Towards eclecticism. In R. A. Dorfman (Ed.), *Paradigms of clinical social work* (pp. 388–412). New York: Brunner/ Mazel.

Rothman, B., & Papell, C. P. (1988). Social group work as a clinical paradigm. In R. A. Dorfman (Ed.), *Paradigms of clinical social work* (pp. 149–178). New York: Brunner/ Mazel.

Rubin, A., & Babbie, E. (1993). *Research methods for social work* (2nd ed.). Pacific Grove, CA: Brooks/Cole.

Saad, J. R. (1984). After ending long-term psychotherapy: Patient reactions in planned and forced termination. (Doctoral dissertation, California School of Professional Psychology, 1983). *Dissertation Abstracts International, 44,* 3541B.

Saari, C. (1991). *The creation of meaning in clinical social work.* New York: Guilford.

Schultz, L. G. (1989). The victimization of social workers. *Journal of Independent Social Work, 3*(3), 51–63.

Schwartz, G. (1989). Confidentiality revisited. *Social Work,*
34(3), 223–226.

Shapiro, J. (1994, April). Subpoenas and patient confidentiality: 'Just tell me what to do.' *NASW California News,* p. 8.

Sheafor, B. W., Horejsi, C. R., & Horejsi, G. A. (1994). *Techniques and guidelines for social work practice* (3rd ed.).
Boston: Allyn and Bacon.

Shulman, L. (1992). *The skills of helping individuals, families,*
and groups (3rd ed.). Itasca, IL: F. E. Peacock.

Simonton, O. C. (1978). *Getting well again.* Los Angeles: J. P.
Tarcher.

Simpson, J. A., & Weiner, E. S. C. (1989). Whistle-blowing. In
Oxford English Dictionary (Vol. XX, 2nd ed.). Oxford:
Clarendon Press.

Siporin, M. (1975). *Introduction to social work practice.* New
York: Macmillan.

Siporin, M. (1982). Moral philosophy for social work today.
Social Service Review, 56, 516–538.

Siporin, M. (1983). Morality and immorality in helping social
work clients. *Social Thought, 9*(4), 10–28.

Siporin, M. (1985). Deviance, morality, and social work therapy.
Social Thought, 11(4), 11–24.

Siporin, M. (1988). Clinical social work as an art form. *Social
Casework, 69,* 177–184.

Siporin, M. (1989). The social work ethic. *Social Thought, 15*(3/
4), 42–52.

Siporin, M. (1993). The social worker's style. *Clinical Social
Work Journal, 21*(3), 257–270.

Slater, S., & Mencher, J. (1991). The lesbian family life cycle: A
contextual approach. *American Journal of Orthopsychiatry,*
61(3), 371–382.

Sluzki, C. E. (1979). Migration and family conflict. *Family
Process, 18*(4), 379–389.

Smalley, R. E. (1970). The functional approach to casework
practice. In R. W. Roberts & R. H. Nee (Eds.), *Theories of
social casework* (pp. 27–28). Chicago: University of Chicago
Press.

Strean, H. S. (1978). *Clinical social work: Theory and practice.*
New York: The Free Press.

Strean, H. S. (1979). *Psychoanalytic theory and social work practice.* New York: The Free Press.

Strean, H. S. (1987). Why therapists lose clients. *Journal of Independent Social Work, 1*(1), 7–17.

Strean, H. S. (1993). *Therapists who have sex with their patients: Treatment and recovery.* New York: Brunner/Mazel.

Strean, H. S. (1994). *Essentials of psychoanalysis.* New York: Brunner/Mazel.

Sue, D. W., & Sue, D. (1990). *Counseling the culturally different: Theory and practice.* New York: John Wiley.

Taft, J. (1937). The relation of function to process in social case work. *Journal of Social Work Process, 1* (3), 1–18. (Reprinted in V. Robinson (Ed.), *Jessie Taft, therapist and social work educator: A professional biography.* (1962). Philadelphia: University of Pennsylvania Press.)

Takeucch, D., Mokuanu, N., & Chun, C. (1992). Services for Asian-Americans and Pacific Islanders. *Journal of Mental Health Administration, 19,* 237–245.

Tammelleo, A. D. (1990). Don't be afraid to blow the whistle on incompetence. *RN, 53*(6), 61–64.

Tarasoff v. Regents of University of California, 12 Ca. App. 3rd 741, 614 P.2d 728 (1976).

Thyer, B. A. (1993). Single-system research designs. In R. M. Grinnell, Jr. (Ed.), *Social work research and evaluation* (4th ed.). Itasca, IL: F. E. Peacock.

Trattner, W. I. (1979). *From Poor Law to welfare state: A history of social welfare in America* (2nd ed.). New York: The Free Press.

Tripodi, T. (1994). *A primer on single-subject design for clinical social workers.* Washington, DC: NASW Press.

Tully, C. T., Kroff, N. P., & Price, J. L. (1991). Is field a hard hat area? A study of violence in field placements. *Journal of Social Work Education, 29*(2), 191–199.

Turner, F. J. (Ed.). (1968). *Differential diagnosis and social work treatment.* New York: The Free Press.

Turner, F. J. (Ed.). (1974). *Social work treatment.* New York: The Free Press.

Turner, F. J. (Ed.). (1976). *Differential diagnosis and treatment in social work* (2nd ed.). New York: The Free Press.

Turner, F. J. (1978). *Psychosocial therapy: A social work perspective.* New York: The Free Press.

Turner, F. J. (Ed.). (1979). *Social work treatment* (2nd ed.). New York: The Free Press.

Turner, F. J. (Ed.). (1983). *Differential diagnosis and social work treatment* (3rd ed.). New York: The Free Press.

Turner, F. J. (Ed.). (1984). *Adult psychopathology.* New York: The Free Press.

Turner, F. J. (Ed.). (1986). *Social work treatment* (3rd ed.). New York: The Free Press.

Turner, F. J. (1988). Psychosocial therapy. In R. A. Dorfman (Ed.), *Paradigms of clinical social work* (pp. 106–122). New York: Brunner/Mazel.

Van Der Bergh, N., & Cooper, L. B. (1987). Feminist social work. In A. Minahan (Ed.), *Encyclopedia of social work* (18th ed., Vol. 1., pp. 610–618). Silver Spring, MD: National Association of Social Workers.

von Bertalanffy, L. (1968). *General systems theory: Foundations, development, applications.* New York: George Braziller.

Walsh, J. (1987). Burnout and values in the social service profession. *Social Casework, 68,* 279–283.

Wapner, J. H., Klein, J. G., Friedlander, M. L., & Andrasik, F. J. (1986). Transferring psychotherapy clients: State of the art. *Professional Psychology: Research and Practice, 17*(6), 492–496.

Watkins, E. C. (1983). Burn-out in counseling practice: Some potential professional and personal hazards of becoming a counselor. *Personnel and Guidance Journal, 61,* 304–308.

Whittaker, J., & Tracy, T. (1989). *Social treatment* (2nd ed.). New York: Aldine.

Wolpe, J. (1985). *Psychotherapy by reciprocal inhibition.* Stanford, CA: Stanford University Press.

Wood, K. M. (1978). Casework effectiveness: A new look at the research evidence. *Social Work, 18,* 437–459.

Woods, M. E., & Hollis, F. (1990). *Casework: A psychosocial therapy* (4th ed.). New York: McGraw-Hill.

Wright, R. (1994). *The moral animal: Evolutionary psychology and everyday life.* New York: Pantheon Books.

Yalom, I. D. (1980). *Existential psychotherapy.* New York: Basic Books.

Yelaja, S. A. (1986). Functional theory for social work practice. In F. Turner (Ed.), *Social work treatment* (3rd ed., pp. 46–68). New York: The Free Press.

NAME INDEX

Addams, Jane, 4–5
Andrasik, F. J., 132, 195
Anna O., 145
Applebaum, P. S., 145, 181
Arches, J., 158, 181
Arndt, B., 115, 187
Aronson, E., 157, 191
Atherton, C. R., 152, 183

Babbie, E., 134, 170, 192
Bandler, B., 25, 181
Barker, R. L., 3, 108, 161, 181
Barlow, D. H., 135, 136, 138,
    181
Bellack, A. S., 139, 187
Bergman, A. S., 50, 181
Bernard, H. S., 168
Bernstein, B., 161, 162, 181
Bloom. M., 134, 135, 136, 138,
    181–182
Blythe, B. J., 135, 138, 139, 143,
    169, 182
Borys, D., 149, 182
Bowen, M., 61, 115, 182
Bowlby, J., 123, 182
Boyd-Franklin N., 63, 182
Branch, T., 159, 191

Breuer, Joseph, 145
Briar, Scott, 20–21, 134, 135, 136,
    138, 143, 169, 182
Brodsky, A., 145, 158, 159, 184
Bullis, R. K., 147, 148, 182
Burke, P., 184
Burns, D. D., 119, 182

Callanan, P., 183
Carter, B., 21, 183
Cash, K., 133
Cherniss, C., 158, 183
Cicchitto, F. R., 121, 183
Chun, C., 33, 194
Clark, L. M., 162, 183
Contro, N. H., 50, 181
Cooper, L. B., 65, 195
Corcoran, K., 75, 139, 167, 184
Corey, G., 149, 183, 186
Corey, M. S., 183
Corsini, R. J., 90, 93, 183
Cowger, C. D., 152, 183

Davis, A. F., 4, 183
Dorfman, R. A., 10, 44, 67, 93, 112,
    116, 169, 183–184
Dubos, Rene, 25, 184

197

SUBJECT INDEX

Page numbers in *italics* refer to illustrations.